Cambridge IGCSE® Chemistry

Practice Book

Bryan Earl and Doug Wilford

AN HACHETTE UK COMPANY

Acknowledgements

The authors would like to thank Irene, Katharine, Michael and Barbara for their patience and encouragement throughout the production of this book. Also to So-Shan and Anne and the publishing team at Hodder Education.

Questions from the Cambridge IGCSE Chemistry papers are reproduced by kind permission of Cambridge International Examinations.

This text has not been through the Cambridge endorsement process.

Although every effort has been made to ensure that website addresses are correct at time of going to press, Hodder Education cannot be held responsible for the content of any website mentioned in this book. It is sometimes possible to find a relocated web page by typing in the address of the home page for a website in the URL window of your browser.

Orders: please contact Bookpoint Ltd, 130 Milton Park, Abingdon, Oxon OX14 4SB. Telephone: (44) 01235 827720; Fax: (44) 01235 400454. Lines are open 9.00–5.00, Monday to Saturday, with a 24-hour message answering service. Visit our website at www.hoddereducation.co.uk.

© Bryan Earl and Doug Wilford 2012

First published in 2012 by

Hodder Education,

An Hachette UK Company

338 Euston Road

London NW1 3BH

Impression number   5   4   3   2   1
Year   2016 2015 2014 2013 2012

All rights reserved. Apart from any use permitted under UK copyright law, no part of this publication may be reproduced or transmitted in any form or by any means, electronic or mechanical, including photocopying and recording, or held within any information storage and retrieval system, without permission in writing from the publisher or under licence from the Copyright Licensing Agency Limited. Further details of such licences (for reprographic reproduction) may be obtained from the Copyright Licensing Agency Limited, Saffron House, 6–10 Kirby Street, London EC1N 8TS.

Cover photo © Andrew Brookes/CORBIS

Typeset in Frutiger 55 Roman 9 points by Datapage (India) Pvt. Ltd.

Printed and bound by CPI Group (UK) Ltd, Croydon, CR0 4YY

A catalogue record for this title is available from the British Library

ISBN: 978 1444 180442

Contents

1 All about matter — 5

2 Elements, compounds and mixtures — 13

3 Atomic structure and the periodic table — 25

4 Bonding and structure — 32

5 Chemical calculations — 43

6 Electrolysis and its uses — 52

7 Acids, bases and salts — 60

8 Inorganic carbon chemistry — 67

9 Metal extraction and chemical reactivity — 76

10 Atmosphere and oceans	84
11 Rates of reaction	95
12 The petroleum industry	107
13 Energy sources	114
14 The (wider) organic manufacturing industry	124
15 Nitrogen	133
16 Sulfur	144
Past exam questions	151

1 All about matter

1 The diagram below shows the different physical changes which can occur between the three states of matter.

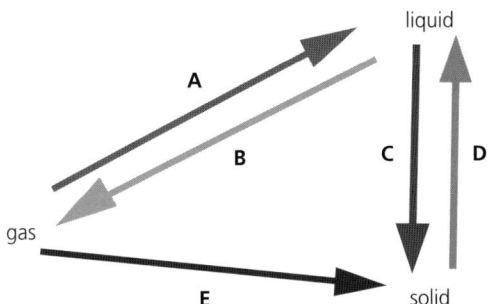

(a) Name the physical changes shown by the letters **A** to **E**.

A ....

B ....

C ....

D ....

E .... (5 marks)

(b) Describe how the particles are arranged and their movement in:

(i) a gas ....

.... (2 marks)

(ii) a liquid ....

.... (3 marks)

(iii) a solid ....

.... (2 marks)

(c) Give an example of a substance which:
(i) undergoes change **E** when heated

.... (1 mark)

(ii) changes from solid to liquid to gas between 0 °C and 100 °C.

.... (1 mark)

5

2 A sample of a solid substance, which had been cooled to −5 °C, was put into a test-tube, which was then heated in a water bath. The temperature of the substance was taken every 5 minutes for an hour. The results obtained are shown below.

Time/min	0	5	10	15	20	25	30	35	40	45	50	55	60
Temperature/°C	−5	−1	5	5	7	13	28	45	62	76	79	82	82

(a) Plot the results on the graph paper below, putting time on the horizontal axis and temperature on the vertical axis.

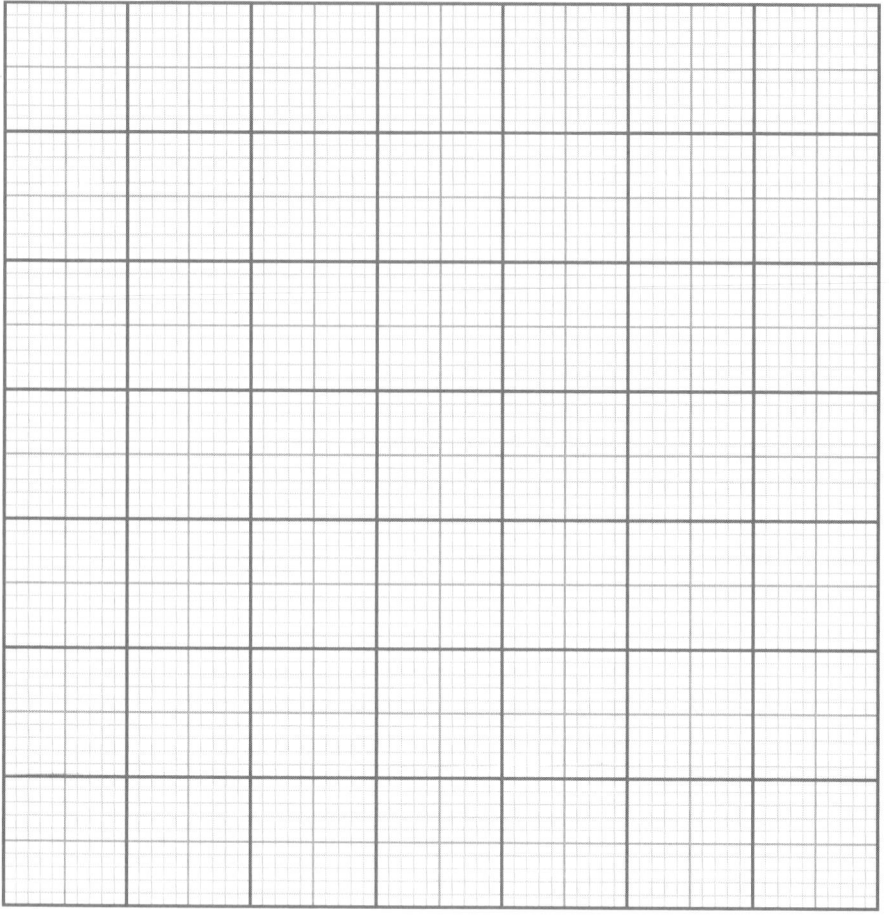

(4 marks)

(b) What is the melting point of the substance? .... (1 mark)

(c) What is the boiling point of the substance? .... (1 mark)

(d) Describe what is happening to the particles of the substance after 50 minutes.

....

.... (2 marks)

3 Imagine that you are a water molecule in an ice cube. Describe what happens to you as the ice cube is heated up to a temperature of 100 °C.

   ....
   ....
   ....
   ....
   ....
   ....
   .... (6 marks)

4 (a) An experiment was carried out which produced a gas as one of the products. On a day when the temperature was 22 °C and the pressure was 1×10^5 Pa, 38 cm³ of the gas was collected after 4 minutes. A repeat of the experiment was carried out the next day to get some repeat results. The pressure was still 1×10^5 Pa but the temperature had increased to 26 °C.

   What volume of gas would be collected, from the same experiment, after 4 minutes on the second day?

   ....
   .... (3 marks)

   (b) Gas from another experiment was collected in a gas syringe. The gas volume, shown by the scale on the syringe, was 75 cm³, measured at 20 °C and 1 atmosphere pressure. If the syringe was sealed and taken outdoors where the temperature was 30 °C, what would the volume rise to? (Assume that the pressure stays the same.)

   ....
   .... (3 marks)

   (c) In an experiment, a student collected 100 cm³ of hydrogen gas at 298 K and 1 atmosphere pressure. What would be the volume of the hydrogen gas if the conditions were changed to 350 K and 2 atmospheres pressure?

   ....
   .... (3 marks)

5 (a) Explain the meaning of each of the following terms.

   (i)   melting ....

   (ii) chemical change ....

   (iii) sublimation ....

   (iv) condensation ....

   (v)   evaporation ....

   (vi) dissolving.. (6 marks)

(b) Which of the terms given in part **(a)** best describes what is taking place in each of the following?

  (i) The formation of water droplets on the inside of a window on a cold day.

  ....

  (ii) The formation of liquid potassium chloride from solid potassium chloride using strong heat.

  ....

  (iii) The formation of iodine vapour from solid iodine on heating.

  ....

  (iv) Adding sugar to hot coffee to sweeten the drink.

  .... (4 marks)

6 Use Charles' Law and Boyle's Law to explain the following.

  (a) In a hospital, a needle and syringe are used to take samples of blood from patients. Explain why blood flows into the syringe when the plunger is pulled back.

  ....

  ....

  ....(2 marks)

  (b) Weather balloons are not completely filled with gas before they are released.

  ....

  ....

  .... (2 marks)

  (c) When de-icer is sprayed from an aerosol can onto ice on a car windscreen, the can gets colder.

  ....

  ....

  .... (2 marks)

  (d) Sea creatures who live thousands of metres under water die if they are caught and brought to the surface.

  ....

  ....

  .... (2 marks)

  (e) In the summer, oil companies change the blend of their petrol mixtures by removing compounds of lower boiling points and replacing them with compounds with higher boiling points.

  ....

  ....

  .... (2 marks)

7 Some liquid bromine was placed in the bottom of a gas jar. The gas jar was then covered by another inverted gas jar and left for several hours.

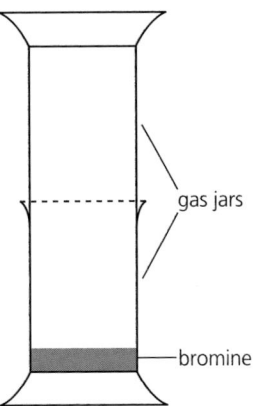

(a) Describe what you would see after:

(i) a few minutes ....

....

(ii) several hours. ....

.... (2 marks)

(b) Explain the answer you have given to part (a) using your ideas of particles.

....

.... (2 marks)

(c) What is the name of the physical process that takes place in this experiment?

.... (1 mark)

(d) What would have been different if the gas jar had been placed in a refrigerator after the bromine had been put into the gas jar? Explain your answer.

....

.... (2 marks)

8 The diagram below shows the arrangement of particles in a solid element which has a melting point of 386 K and a boiling point of 718 K. Using the boxes below, draw diagrams to show the arrangement of the particles in the element at 400 K and 750 K.

298 K   400 K   750 K

(4 marks)

Stretch and challenge

9 When the following experiment is set up, a cloud of fine white powder can be seen as the ammonia gas reacts with the hydrogen chloride gas.

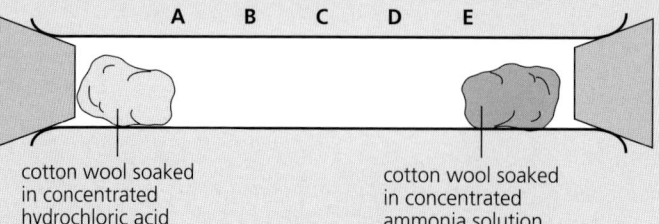

cotton wool soaked in concentrated hydrochloric acid

cotton wool soaked in concentrated ammonia solution

Hydrogen chloride particles are more than twice as heavy as ammonia particles.

(a) Which of the particles will move faster?

.... (1 mark)

(b) At which point, **A** to **E**, along the tube will the white cloud be seen? Explain your answer in terms of the movement of the particles.

....

....

.... (2 marks)

(c) How do the particles of hydrogen chloride and ammonia gas move along the tube?

.... (1 mark)

Exam focus

1 (a) (i) Give two properties shown by:

a solid ....

....

a liquid ....

....

a gas. ....

.... [6]

(ii) Draw diagrams in the boxes below to show how the particles are arranged in each of the physical states.

| solid | liquid | gas | [3] |

(b) The melting and boiling points of five substances are given in the table below.

Substance	Melting point/K	Boiling point/K
Oxygen	55	90
Bromine	266	332
Mercury	234	630
Phosphorus	317	553
Iron	1808	3023

(Take room temperature as 298 K.)

(i) What is the melting point of mercury in °C? ....

(ii) Which element(s) is a gas at room temperature? ....

(iii) Which element(s) is a solid at room temperature? ....

(iv) Which of the elements will boil first if the temperature is raised from room

temperature? .... [4]

[Total: 13]

2 Use the kinetic theory to explain the following.

(a) Walking along the street in front of a coffee shop, it is possible to smell the coffee.

....

....

.... [2]

(b) When laying railway track, gaps have to be left between the lengths of track.

....

....

.... [2]

(c) When a tea bag is placed in a cup of hot water, the colour of the water changes.

....

....

.... [2]

(d) In the winter months, the amount of water found running down the inside of windows increases.

....

....

.... [2]

(e) A bubble of methane rises from the bottom of the Pacific Ocean. As it rises, the bubble gets bigger.

....

....

.... [2]

(f) Pollen grains are mixed with water and observed under a microscope. Dust particles in the air are also observed in the same way.

  (i) What would the pollen grains and dust particles be doing?

  .... [1]

  (ii) What causes the grains and dust particles to behave in the way you have described in part **(i)**?

  ....

  .... [2]

[Total: 13]

2 Elements, compounds and mixtures

1 (a) Elements are the basic building blocks of the universe. What do you understand scientifically by the term *element*?

....
.... (3 marks)

(b) More than 110 elements have now been identified, including the following:

astatine	bromine	calcium	carbon	chlorine
hydrogen	lead	magnesium	mercury	oxygen
	phosphorus	silver	sodium	zinc

Elements can be divided into *metals* and *non-metals*. Which of the elements above are:

(i) metals? ....

....

(ii) non-metals? ....

.... (14 marks)

(c) Complete the following paragraphs about metal and non-metal elements by writing in words from the lists below.

(i) | ductile good high liquid lustrous malleable solids |

Metals have .... melting points, boiling points

and densities. Metals are .... conductors of

heat and electricity. They are usually ...., except

in the case of mercury, which is a .... at room

temperature. They are .... as well as easy to

draw into wires (...). Metals are generally

shiny (...). (7 marks)

(ii) | brittle densities dull gases insulators low poor |

Non-metal elements have .... melting points,

boiling points and .... Non-metals are

.... conductors of heat and electricity, and

often they are .... Non-metals are not easily

made into wires because they are .... or soft

solids, liquids or .... When in the solid form

they are .... (7 marks)

13

2 Complete the table below, writing in either the symbol or the name of the element.

Element	Symbol
Argon	
	F
Copper	
	Ni
Silicon	
	K
Helium	
	Sn
Krypton	
	Al

(10 marks)

3 The table below shows the melting points, boiling points and densities of elements E to I.

Substance	Melting point/°C	Boiling point/°C	Density/g cm^{-3}
E	−259	−253	0.09
F	1085	2580	8.93
G	−7	59	3.1
H	−39	357	13.6
I	−218	−183	0.0013

(a) Which of these substances, E to I, are gases at room temperature?

.... (2 marks)

(b) Which of these substances, E to I, are liquids at room temperature?

.... (2 marks)

(c) Which of these substances, E to I, are solids at room temperature?

.... (1 mark)

(d) Which of these substances, E to I, are most likely to be metals?

.... (2 marks)

(e) Which of these substances, E to I, is most likely to be mercury?

.... (1 mark)

(f) Which of these substances, E to I, is the least dense metal?

.... (1 mark)

(g) Which of these substances, E to I, will be a liquid at −210 °C?

.... (1 mark)

(h) Which of these substances, E to I, are gases at 65 °C?

.... (3 marks)

(i) Which of these substances, E to I, is most likely to be bromine?

.... (1 mark)

(j) Which of these substances, E to I, is the least dense non-metal?

.... (1 mark)

4 (a) Pick the 'odd one out' in each of the following groups of elements and explain why it is different from the others.

  (i) Cu, C, Ca, Cs, Cr

  Odd one out ....

  Explanation .... (2 marks)

  (ii) nitrogen, neon, sulfur, iron, silicon

  Odd one out ....

  Explanation .... (2 marks)

  (iii) Mg, Al, Cl, Na, Ar

  Odd one out ....

  Explanation .... (2 marks)

(b) For each of the following statements about elements, write either 'true' or 'false'.

  (i) There are only 103 elements. .... (1 mark)

  (ii) More elements are metals than non-metals. .... (1 mark)

  (iii) Each element has a chemical name and a symbol. .... (1 mark)

  (iv) Metals such as magnesium contain two atoms joined together

  to form molecules. .... (1 mark)

  (v) Molecules of argon contain only one atom. .... (1 mark)

  (vi) Some of the symbols for the elements come from their Chinese

  names. .... (1 mark)

  (vii) Where elements contain two atoms joined together in pairs, they are called

  diatomic. .... (1 mark)

5 (a) Distinguish between the terms *compound* and *mixture*, using specific examples.

....

.... (3 marks)

(b) Here is a list of substances:

> beer   brass   carbon monoxide   cement
> lemonade   limestone   methane   sodium hydroxide
> stainless steel   sulfuric acid

Which of these substances are:

  (i) compounds? ....

  ....

  (ii) mixtures? ....

  .... (10 marks)

(c) Pick the 'odd one out' in each of the following groups and explain why it is different from the others.

  (i) petrol, oil, water, air, solder

  Odd one out ....

  Explanation .... (2 marks)

(ii) lead nitrate, potassium oxide, chromium, hydrochloric acid, sand

Odd one out ....

Explanation .... (2 marks)

(iii) HCl, F_2, MgO, FeS, CO_2

Odd one out ....

Explanation .... (2 marks)

(d) There are many types of mixtures, including gels, emulsions and foams. They are made by mixing different combinations of solids, liquids and gases.
  (i) Complete the table below.

Example	Type of mixture	Mixture made from
Bread		
Mayonnaise		
Jelly		

(6 marks)

(ii) Describe the difference between a foam and an emulsion.

....

.... (3 marks)

6 (a) A mixture of zinc metal powder and sulfur was heated strongly in a test-tube. A bright red glow spread very quickly throughout the mixture during the reaction. At the end of the experiment, a white powder was produced.
  (i) What safety precautions should be taken when carrying out this experiment?

.... (2 marks)

(ii) Explain what the 'bright red glow' indicates. ....

.... (1 mark)

(iii) Give the chemical name of the 'white powder'. ....

....(1 mark)

(iv) Write a word equation and a balanced chemical equation for the reaction which has taken place.

....

.... (3 marks)

(v) The white solid is a compound. Explain the difference between the mixture of zinc and sulfur and the compound formed by the chemical reaction between them.

....

.... (3 marks)

(vi) Many compounds are very useful substances. Salt (chemical name sodium chloride) is one of these useful compounds. It is a white crystalline solid and has been prized by people for a very long time. Find and make a list of the things that we use salt for in our world today.

....

.... (3 marks)

(b) The metal copper can be extracted from its ore, copper sulfide, in a two-stage process:

    I   Copper sulfide reacts with oxygen at a high temperature to form copper oxide and sulfur dioxide gas.

    II Then the copper oxide is reacted with carbon, again at high temperature, to form copper metal and carbon dioxide gas.

  (i) Name the elements mentioned in the passage above.

.... (2 marks)

  (ii) Name the compounds mentioned in the passage above.

....

.... (4 marks)

  (iii) Write word and balanced chemical equations for the reactions described in the passage above.

....

....

....

.... (8 marks)

7 (a) The table on page 18 shows the formulae for some compounds.
Complete the table by writing in:
  (i) the symbols present in each formula and the elements they represent
  (ii) the number of atoms of each element present in the formula
  (iii) the total number of atoms present in the formula.

The first one has been done for you.   (1 mark for each correct answer)

(b) Balance the following equations.

  (i) $Pb(s) + O_2(g) \rightarrow PbO(s)$

.... (2 marks)

  (ii) $H_2(g) + O_2(g) \rightarrow H_2O(l)$

.... (2 marks)

  (iii) $C_2H_4(g) + O_2(g) \rightarrow CO_2(g) + H_2O(l)$

.... (2 marks)

  (iv) $Fe(s) + Br_2(l) \rightarrow FeBr_3(s)$

.... (2 marks)

  (v) $CuO(s) + HCl(aq) \rightarrow CuCl_2(aq) + H_2O(l)$

.... (2 marks)

  (vi) $SnO_2(s) + H_2(g) \rightarrow Sn(s) + H_2O(l)$

.... (2 marks)

  (vii) $KOH(aq) + H_3PO_4(aq) \rightarrow K_3PO_4(aq) + H_2O(l)$

.... (2 marks)

  (viii) $ZnO(s) + HCl(aq) \rightarrow ZnCl_2(aq) + H_2O(l)$

.... (2 marks)

  (ix) $CuO(s) + NH_3(g) \rightarrow N_2(g) + Cu(s) + H_2O(l)$

.... (2 marks)

  (x) $Pb(NO_3)_2(s) \rightarrow PbO(s) + NO_2(g) + O_2(g)$

.... (2 marks)

ELEMENTS, COMPOUNDS AND MIXTURES

Formula of substance	Elements present			Total number of atoms
	Symbol	Name	Number of atoms	
NaNO$_3$	Na	Sodium	1	5
	N	Nitrogen	1	
	O	Oxygen	3	
LiNO$_3$				
CaCO$_3$				
Mg$_3$N$_2$				
Ag$_2$CrO$_4$				
AlBr$_4$Cs				
NH$_4$CO$_2$NH$_2$				
NaAuCl$_4$				

8 (a) The diagram below shows the apparatus used for fractional distillation. The labels have been replaced with numbers.

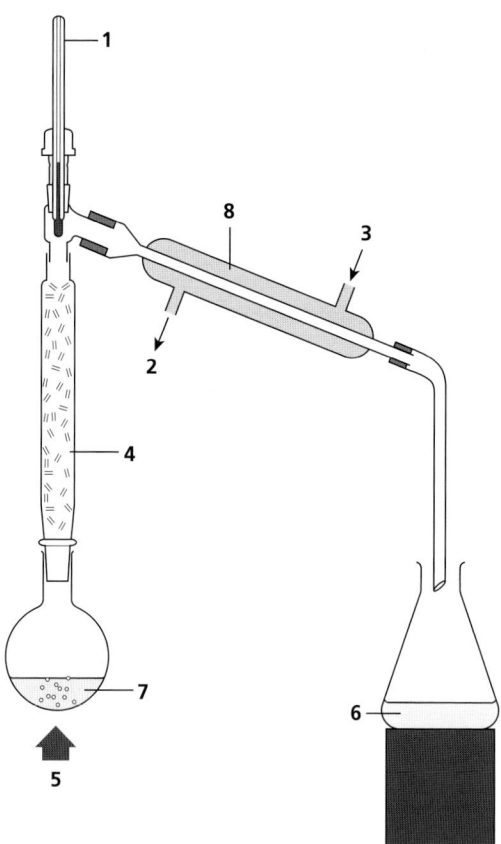

(i) For each number, write down the correct label from the list below.

cold water in	cold water out	distillate
fractionating column	heat	Liebig condenser
	mixture of liquids	thermometer

1 ....
2 ....
3 ....
4 ....
5 ....
6 ....
7 ....
8 .... (8 marks)

(ii) Which of the following mixtures can be separated successfully by fractional distillation? Explain your answers.

```
crude oil   magnesium and sulfur
   a mixture of dyes   air
```

....
....
....
.... (4 marks)

(b) The diagram below shows a simple apparatus used for chromatography. The labels have been replaced with numbers.
For each number, write down the correct label from the list below.

```
pencil line   beaker   solvent
samples   chromatography paper
```

1 ....
2 ....
3 ....
4 ....
5 .... (5 marks)

(c) The next part of this question is about the properties of some materials. The table below gives information about four materials: nylon, Kevlar, polythene and carbon-reinforced plastic.

Material	Relative heaviness	Relative strength	Relative stiffness	Relative cost
Nylon	1100	8	3	Medium
Kevlar	1500	300	190	Very high
Polythene	960	2.0	0.6	Low
Carbon-reinforced plastic	1600	180	200	High

(i) Using the relative values shown in the table and your knowledge of materials generally, describe and explain two reasons for using polythene in packaging.

.... (2 marks)

(ii) A large materials company won a contract to make bulletproof vests for the police. Using information from the table above, suggest which material they should use for this purpose and explain your answer.

....
.... (3 marks)

(iii) Carbon-reinforced plastic is a composite material. What is meant by the term *composite material*?

....
.... (2 marks)

Stretch and challenge

9 The metal zinc can be extracted from its ore, zinc sulfide (zinc blende), in a two-stage process. The second part of the process involves a *redox* reaction in which zinc oxide is reacted with carbon, at a high temperature, to form zinc metal and carbon monoxide gas.

   zinc oxide + coke (carbon) → zinc + carbon monoxide

   (a) What do you understand by the term *redox*?

   .... (2 marks)

   (b) Which of the substances shown in the word equation is being:

   (i) oxidised? .... (1 mark)

   (ii) reduced? .... (1 mark)

   Which of the substances shown in the word equation is acting as the:

   (iii) oxidising agent? .... (1 mark)

   (iv) reducing agent? .... (1 mark)

   (c) Write a balanced chemical equation for the reaction shown in the word equation.

   .... (3 marks)

   (d) The word equations below describe reactions by which the metals lead and tin are obtained from their ores.

   lead oxide + carbon → lead + carbon dioxide
   tin(IV) oxide + hydrogen gas → tin + water

   In each of these reactions, which of the substances shown is being:

   (i) oxidised? .... (2 marks)

   (ii) reduced? .... (2 marks)

   Which of the substances shown is acting as the:

   (iii) oxidising agent? .... (2 marks)

   (iv) reducing agent? .... (2 marks)

   (v) Write a balanced chemical equation for each of these reactions.

   ....

   .... (3 marks each)

Stretch and challenge

10 Forensic scientists recovered several samples from a crime scene. Chromatography was carried out on these samples. The scientists placed the samples onto chromatography paper. The chromatogram produced was sprayed with a *locating agent*.
The R_f *values* were then measured for each of the samples taken.

(a) What do you understand by the term:

(i) locating agent? ....
.... (2 marks)

(ii) R_f value? ....
.... (2 marks)

(b) The samples were thought to be amino acids. Use your research skills to find out the normal locating agent used for amino acids.
.... (1 mark)

(c) The table below shows R_f values for several amino acids thought to be at the crime scene, and for three samples.

Amino acid	R_f value
Alanine	0.65
Glycine	0.25
Threonine	0.57
Proline	0.60
Lysine	0.16
Methionine	0.50
Sample 1	0.64
Sample 2	0.18
Sample 3	0.24

(i) Identify the samples taken from the crime scene using the data from the table.

Sample 1 ....

Sample 2 ....

Sample 3 .... (3 marks)

(ii) Explain how you made your choices in part **(i)**.
.... (1 mark)

Exam focus

1 Iron is usually extracted from its ore haematite (iron(III) oxide). The following is a brief outline of the reactions involved in this extraction.

    I   coke + oxygen → carbon dioxide
    II carbon dioxide + coke → carbon monoxide
    III iron(III) oxide + carbon monoxide → iron + carbon dioxide

(a) Write balanced chemical equations for:
    (i) reaction I
    .... [2]
    (ii) reaction II.
    .... [3]

(b) Which substance is being oxidised in reaction I? .... [1]

(c) Which substance is being reduced in reaction II? .... [1]

(d) Balance the following equation for reaction III.

$$Fe_2O_3(s) + CO(g) \rightarrow Fe(l) + CO_2(g)$$

    .... [2]

(e) In reaction III, which substance is acting as the reducing agent and which is acting as the oxidising agent?

    .... [2]

(f) Complete the table below.

Formula of substance	Elements present			Total number of atoms
	Name	Symbol	Number of atoms	
Fe_2O_3				
CO				
Fe				
CO_2				

[25]

(g) Which of the substances shown in the table are:

    (i) elements? ....

    (ii) compounds? .... [4]

[Total: 40]

2 The table below shows some information about four different elements, **W, X, Y** and **Z**. (Note that **W, X, Y** and **Z** are *not* chemical symbols.)

(a) Complete the following table.

Element	Metal or non-metal?	Shiny?	Conductor of electricity?	Melting point
W	Metal		Yes	High
X	Non-metal	No	No	Low
Y		Yes	Yes	High
Z	Non-metal	No		Low

[3]

(b) Zinc is a metal. Give **one** property of zinc, *not shown in the table,* which shows that it is a metal. .... [1]

(c) Fireworks were invented by the Chinese centuries ago. There are many different types of fireworks, including bangers, Roman candles, rockets and sparklers. Sparklers usually consist of a chemical mixture that has been moulded onto a thin wire. One of the main substances found in the mixture is iron powder.

The word equation for one of the main reactions that takes place during the burning of a sparkler is:

iron + oxygen → iron oxide

(i) Give the name of one of the *reactants* present in the word equation above. .... [1]

(ii) Give the name of the *compound* present in the word equation above. .... [1]

(iii) Give **one** reason why people should be careful when handling sparklers. .... [1]

(iv) Write a balanced chemical equation for the reaction of iron with oxygen.

.... [3]

[Total: 10]

3 Atomic structure and the periodic table

1 Element **Y** has a proton number of 19 and a relative atomic mass of 39.
   (a) (i) How many electrons, protons and neutrons are there in an atom of element **Y**?
   .... (3 marks)
   (ii) What is the electronic configuration of this element?
   .... (1 mark)
   (iii) In which group of the periodic table would you find this element? Explain your answer.
   .... (2 marks)
   (iv) What would be the symbol for the ion which element **Y** forms?
   .... (1 mark)

   (b) The proton number of bromine (Br) is 35. It is in Group 7 of the periodic table – it is a halogen. How many electrons will bromine have in its outer energy level?
   .... (1 mark)

   (c) When potassium metal is heated and lowered into a gas jar of bromine vapour, a chemical reaction occurs which produces white fumes.
   (i) What do the white fumes consist of?
   .... (1 mark)
   (ii) Write word and balanced chemical equations for the reaction.
   ....
   .... (4 marks)
   (iii) When potassium is reacted with chlorine gas, the reaction is more vigorous. Explain this observation in terms of the reactivity of the halogens.
   ....
   ....
   ....
   ....
   .... (3 marks)

2 Use the information given in the table below to answer the following questions about elements **A, B, C, D** and **E**.

Element	Proton number	Nucleon number	Electronic structure
A	10	20	2,8
B	19	39	2,8,8,1
C	13	27	
D	8	16	
E		35	2,8,7

(a) Complete the table by writing in:
  (i) the electronic structure of elements **C** and **D** (2 marks)
  (ii) the proton number of element **E**. (1 mark)

(b) (i) Which of these elements, **A** to **E**, is a noble gas? .... (1 mark)

  (ii) Which of these elements, **A** to **E**, is a Group 1 element? .... (1 mark)

  (iii) Which of these elements, **A** to **E**, is a Group 7 element? .... (1 mark)

  (iv) Which of these elements, **A** to **E**, is aluminium? .... (1 mark)

(c) (i) Which of these elements, **A** to **E**, will form an ion with a +3 charge?
  .... (1 mark)

  (ii) Which of these elements, **A** to **E**, will form an ion with a –2 charge?
  .... (1 mark)

  (iii) Which of these elements, **A** to **E**, will not form an ion?
  .... (1 mark)

3 The diagram below shows part of the periodic table.

1	2											3	4	5	6	7	0
													H				
												C	N		F	Ne	
Na	Mg											Al		P	S		
	Ca				Mn											Br	Kr

Using the elements shown above, write down the symbol for an element which:

(a) is a transition element ....

(b) has four electrons in its outer energy level ....

(c) is a liquid at room temperature and pressure ....

(d) is stored under oil ....

(e) has a full outer electron energy level ....

(f) has an electronic configuration of 2,8,5 ....

(g) is a Group 1 metal ....

(h) is a gaseous Group 7 element. .... (8 marks)

4 There are five elements in Group 7 of the periodic table. They are known as the halogens. The table below gives the melting and boiling points of the halogens. However, one of the values is missing.

Element	Atomic number	Melting point/K	Boiling point/K
F	9	54	85
Cl	17	172	239
Br	35	266	
I	53	387	458
At	85	576	610

(a) Plot a graph of the melting and boiling points of the halogens against their atomic number. Join the plotted points for the melting points together and, in a different colour, the plotted points for the boiling points.

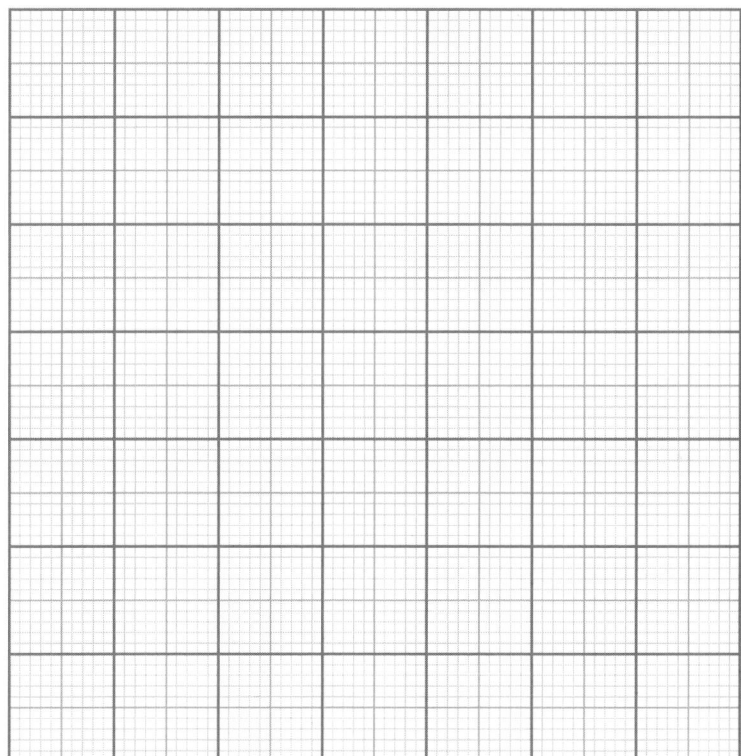

(6 marks)

(b) Use your graph to estimate the boiling point of bromine. .... (1 mark)

(c) What is the trend in the melting points of the halogens?

.... (1 mark)

(d) Which of the halogens would be a gas at room temperature (298 K)?

.... (2 marks)

5 Copper, element 29 in the periodic table, is found as two isotopes: ^{63}Cu (69.1%) and ^{65}Cu (30.9%).

(a) Complete the table below to show the numbers of electrons, protons and neutrons in each of the isotopes of copper. (2 marks)

Isotope	Number of		
	Electrons	Protons	Neutrons
^{63}Cu			
^{65}Cu			

(b) What are *isotopes*?

....

.... (2 marks)

(c) What is the relative atomic mass (A_r) of an element?

....

.... (2 marks)

(d) Calculate the relative atomic mass (A_r) of copper from the information given.

....

.... (2 marks)

6 Chlorine gas will react with aluminium metal using the apparatus shown below.

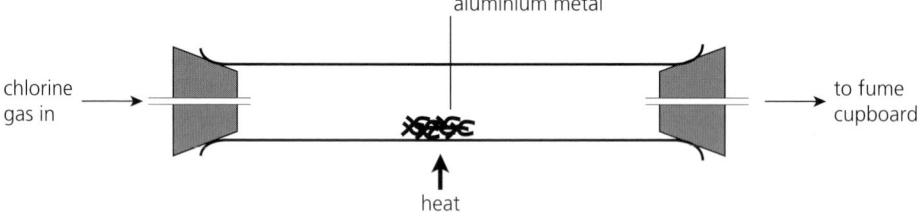

(a) Write word and balanced chemical equations for the reaction between aluminium metal and chlorine gas.

....

.... (4 marks)

(b) Why is it necessary to ensure that the unreacted chlorine gas is passed into a fume cupboard?

.... (1 mark)

(c) Name a halogen which would react with aluminium metal more quickly than

chlorine does. .... (1 mark)

(d) Name a metal which would react with chlorine gas more quickly than aluminium

does. .... (1 mark)

ATOMIC STRUCTURE AND THE PERIODIC TABLE

7   In 1817, Johann Döbereiner tried to organise the elements that were known at that time into an order which would be useful to other chemists. He put elements into groups of three called 'triads'. One of these groups contained the elements lithium, sodium and potassium.

(a) Describe how the reactions of these elements with water are:

(i) similar ....

....

.... (4 marks)

(ii) different. ....

....

.... (2 marks)

Explain your answers in terms of the electronic structure and/or size of the atoms of the elements.

(b) In another group Döbereiner placed the elements strontium, barium and calcium.

(i) In which group of the modern periodic table will you find these

elements? .... (1 mark)

(ii) How many electrons will each of these elements have in its outer energy

level? .... (1 mark)

(iii) Which of these elements will undergo the most vigorous reaction when added to water? Explain your answer in terms of its electronic structure.

....

....

.... (3 marks)

8   Complete the following passage.

The modern periodic table has been credited to the work of the Russian chemist

.... After many years of chemists across the world trying to classify the elements in a useful way, he came up with the table which we have been using for nearly 150 years. He arranged the elements in order of increasing

.... Occasionally he had to swap elements around so

that they were in the same .... as other elements with

similar properties, for example tellurium (Te) and ....

(...................). The major change that he introduced to his classification was that he

left .... for elements which had not been discovered at the time.

Today the elements in the modern periodic table are arranged in order of

increasing ....   (6 marks)

29

Stretch and challenge

9 The diagram below shows the elements in Period 3 of the periodic table.

| Na | Mg |

| Al | Si | P | S | Cl | Ar |

(a) Moving across Period 3, what happens to the metallic character of the elements?
.... (1 mark)

(b) In how many energy levels do all these elements have electrons?
.... (1 mark)

(c) (i) How many electrons does a magnesium atom have? .... (1 mark)

(ii) What charge does a magnesium ion have? .... (1 mark)

(d) Which of the elements in Period 3 will form ions with a negative charge? .... (2 marks)

(e) Argon is called a noble, or inert, gas.
(i) What is meant by the term *inert*?
.... (1 mark)

(ii) Explain why argon is inert.
....
.... (2 marks)

(iii) Give a use for argon. .... (1 mark)

■ *Exam focus*

1 Displacement reactions occur when a solution containing a halide ion reacts with a more reactive halogen. This type of reaction can be seen when a solution of potassium bromide reacts with chlorine.

   (a) Write word and balanced chemical equations for the reaction which occurs between potassium bromide solution and chlorine.

   .... [1]

   .... [3]

   (b) Why is chlorine more reactive than bromine? ....

   ....

   .... [2]

   (c) Which other halogen would react with potassium bromide? .... [1]

   (d) Would there be a reaction between a solution of sodium fluoride and bromine? Explain your answer.

   ....

   .... [2]

   [Total: 9]

2 In the periodic table, elements are arranged in vertical columns called groups. Within each group, the elements have similar chemical reactions but show a trend in their physical properties such as reactivity and melting point.

   (a) Consider the two elements potassium and sodium, both found in Group 1 of the periodic table.

      (i) Give the electronic configurations of the elements sodium and potassium.

          .... [2]

      (ii) Which of these elements, potassium or sodium, is the more reactive when added to water? Explain your answer in terms of their atomic structure.

          .... [2]

      (iii) Write a balanced chemical equation for the reaction of sodium with water.

          .... [3]

   (b) In Group 7 there are five elements, all of which have the same number of electrons in their outer energy level.

      (i) How many electrons do these elements have in their outer energy

         level? .... [1]

      (ii) What do all of these elements do when they react and form ions?

          .... [1]

      (iii) What would be the charge on an ion of any of the Group 7 ions? .... [1]

      (iv) Which of the Group 7 elements would be the most reactive? Explain your answer.

          ....

          .... [3]

   [Total: 13]

4 Bonding and structure

1 Draw diagrams to show the bonding in each of the following ionic compounds.
   (a) lithium chloride (LiCl)

   (4 marks)

   (b) calcium sulfide (CaS)

   (4 marks)

   (c) potassium oxide (K$_2$O)

   (4 marks)

(d) aluminium fluoride (AlF$_3$)

(4 marks)

2 For each of the following statements about ionic bonding and ionic compounds, write either 'true' or 'false'.

(a) Ionic bonds are formed between non-metals only. .... (1 mark)

(b) Ionic bonds are formed by transfer of electrons between the elements forming the bond. .... (1 mark)

(c) Ionic compounds usually have low melting points and high boiling points. .... (1 mark)

(d) Ionic compounds contain charged particles called ions. .... (1 mark)

(e) Generally, ionic compounds are hard solids. .... (1 mark)

(f) Generally, ionic compounds cannot conduct electricity when solid because the ions are not free to move. .... (1 mark)

3 (a) The table below shows the valencies of some common ions.

	Valency		
	1	2	3
Metals	Sodium (Na$^+$)	Magnesium (Mg^{2+})	Aluminium (Al^{3+})
	Potassium (K$^+$)	Lead (Pb^{2+})	Iron (Fe^{3+})
	Silver (Ag$^+$)	Barium (Ba^{2+})	
Non-metals	Fluoride (F$^-$)	Oxide (O^{2-})	
	Chloride (Cl$^-$)	Sulfide (S^{2-})	
	Bromide (Br$^-$)		
Groups of atoms	Hydroxide (OH$^-$)	Carbonate (CO$_3^{2-}$)	Phosphate (PO$_4^{3-}$)
	Nitrate (NO$_3^-$)	Sulfate (SO$_4^{2-}$)	
	Ammonium (NH$_4^+$)		

Use the information in the table to work out the formula of each of the following compounds.

(i) potassium chloride .... (1 mark)

(ii) copper(II) fluoride .... (1 mark)

(iii) sodium carbonate .... (1 mark)

(iv) silver phosphate .... (1 mark)

(v) lead oxide .... (1 mark)

(vi) ammonium sulfate .... (1 mark)

(vii) magnesium phosphate .... (1 mark)

(viii) barium sulfide .... (1 mark)

(ix) aluminium hydroxide .... (1 mark)

(x) iron(III) bromide .... (1 mark)

(b) Using the formulae from your answers to part (a), give the ratio of the atoms present for each of those compounds.

(i) ....

(ii) ....

(iii) ....

(iv) ....

(v) ....

(vi) ....

(vii) ....

(viii) ....

(ix) ....

(x) ....

(10 marks)

4 Draw diagrams to show the bonding in each of the following covalent compounds.

(a) hydrogen fluoride (HF)

(4 marks)

(b) nitrogen trichloride (NCl$_3$)

(4 marks)

(c) dichlorodifluoromethane (CCl$_2$F$_2$)

(4 marks)

(d) ethyne (C$_2$H$_2$)

(4 marks)

5 For each of the following statements about covalent bonding and covalent compounds, write either 'true' or 'false'.

(a) Covalent bonds are formed between non-metals only. .... (1 mark)

(b) Covalent bonds are formed by sharing of electrons between the elements forming the bond. .... (1 mark)

(c) Covalent compounds usually have low melting and boiling points.

.... (1 mark)

(d) Simple covalent substances are often soft or waxy solids. .... (1 mark)

(e) Generally, covalent compounds conduct electricity when molten or dissolved in water. .... (1 mark)

(f) Generally, covalent compounds do not dissolve in water. .... (1 mark)

6 The table below shows the melting and boiling points of some substances.

Substance	Melting point/°C	Boiling point/°C
Sulfur dioxide	−73	−10
Copper(II) chloride	620	993
Barium chloride	963	1560
Ethanol	−117	78
Hexane	−95	69
Aluminium oxide	2072	2980
Potassium chloride	770	1500
Ammonia	−77	−34
Lead sulfide	1118	1344
Tin(IV) chloride	−33	114

(a) Which of the substances in the table are most likely to be:
  (i) covalent substances?

  ....
  .... (4 marks)

  (ii) ionic substances?

  ....
  .... (6 marks)

  (iii) Explain your answers to parts (i) and (ii).

  ....
  ....
  ....
  .... (4 marks)

(b) At room temperature, which of the covalent substances in the table will be:
(i) gases?
....
....
(ii) liquids?
....
.... (4 marks)

(c) (i) Which substance in the table would you expect to be ionic, but from its data appears to be covalent in character? .... (1 mark)

(ii) Explain the reasoning behind your answer to part (i).
....
.... (2 marks)

7 Here is a list of substances:

> ammonia   carbon dioxide   chlorine   copper(II) sulfate
> fluorine   gold   iron(II) oxide   hydrogen   hydrogen chloride
> lead nitrate   lithium   magnesium   nickel(II) bromide
> nitrogen   oxygen   sodium chloride   sulfur trioxide
> tin   titanium   water

Which of these substances are:

(a) covalent elements? ....
.... (5 marks)

(b) metallic elements? ....
.... (5 marks)

(c) covalent compounds? ....
.... (5 marks)

(d) ionic compounds? ....
.... (5 marks)

8 The diagrams below show two different forms of carbon, **A** and **B**.

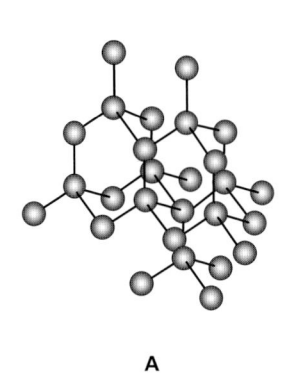

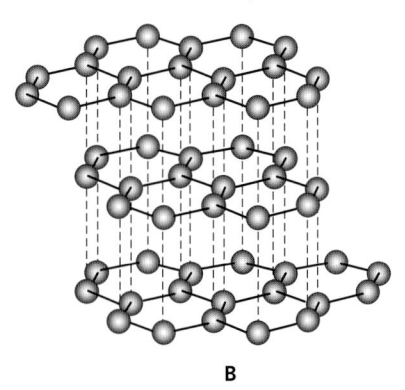

A   B

(a) Name the two allotropes of carbon shown above.

.... (2 marks)

(b) Explain the meaning of the term *allotrope*.

....

.... (2 marks)

(c) (i) What type of bonding is represented by these forms of carbon?

.... (1 mark)

(ii) What type of structure is represented by these forms of carbon?

.... (1 mark)

(d) (i) How many carbon atoms are linked to each other carbon atom in form **A**? .... (1 mark)

(ii) How many carbon atoms are linked to each other carbon atom in form **B**? .... (1 mark)

(e) Complete the table below, which relates to the properties of the metal copper and substances **A** and **B**.

Substance	Electrical conductivity	Melting point	Hardness
Copper	Good	High	High
A			
B			

(6 marks)

(f) In 1985, a new allotrope of carbon was discovered. What is the name of this allotrope? .... (1 mark)

Stretch and challenge

9 Silicon(IV) oxide has a structure similar to that of diamond, in which each silicon atom is attached to four oxygen atoms.

(a) Draw a rough sketch to show the structure of silicon(IV) oxide.

(2 marks)

(b) What type of bonding would you expect to find in the compound silicon(IV) oxide? .... (1 mark)

(c) Explain why silicon(IV) oxide:
  (i) is a hard substance
  ....
  .... (2 marks)
  (ii) does not conduct electricity
  ....
  .... (2 marks)
  (iii) has a high melting point.
  ....
  .... (2 marks)

Stretch and challenge

10 (a) The bonding in metals can be described in the following way:

'It is an electrostatic force of attraction between free electrons and the regular array of positive metal ions within the solid metal. The bonding in metals gives rise to certain properties.'

Complete the following passage about the properties of metals by writing in words from the list.

| attractive | conductors | delocalised | ductile | energy |
| energy levels | high | ions | malleable | negative |

Metals are good .... of electricity and heat, because the free electrons from the outer .... of metal atoms carry a .... charge or heat .... through the metal. The free electrons are often described as .... The free electrons allow metal .... to slide over each other, so metals are .... and ....

They have .... melting and boiling points due to the strong .... forces within the structure of the metal.

(10 marks)

(b) The melting point of calcium (840 °C) is much higher than that of potassium (63 °C). Using the idea of metallic bonding, explain why this is the case.

....

....

....

....

....

.... (4 marks)

Exam focus

1 The diagram below shows the structure of sodium chloride (salt).

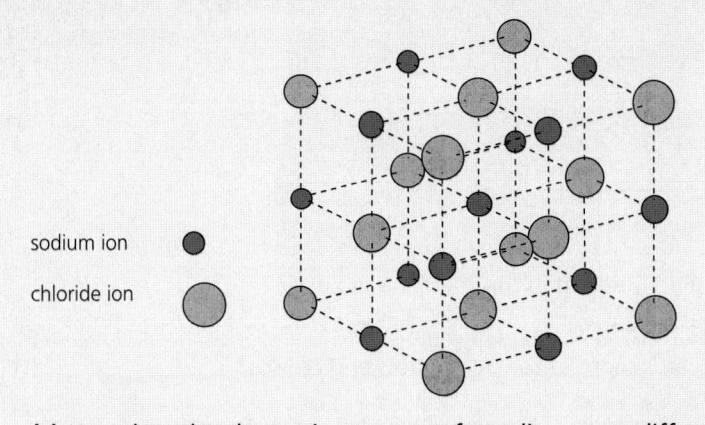

sodium ion ●

chloride ion ○

(a) How does the electronic structure of a sodium atom differ from that of a sodium ion?

....

.... [2]

(b) How does the electronic structure of a chlorine atom differ from that of a chloride ion?

....

....

.... [2]

(c) What type of chemical bond is found in sodium chloride?

.... [1]

(d) Using the diagram of sodium chloride above, explain why sodium chloride:
  (i) crystals are cubic in shape

  ....

  .... [2]

  (ii) has a high melting point (801 °C)

  ....

  .... [2]

  (iii) acts as an insulator when solid, but will conduct electricity when molten.

  ....

  .... [2]

[Total: 11]

2 One of our most important fuels is natural gas (methane, CH_4). The diagram below shows the bonding in a methane molecule.

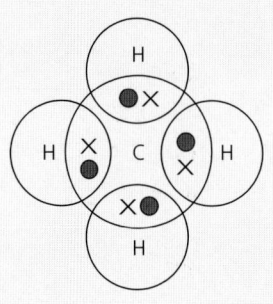

(a) What type of bonding is shown in this methane molecule?

.... [2]

(b) What type of particle is represented by the dots and crosses?

.... [1]

(c) Methane is a gas at room temperature and pressure. Explain why this is the case.

....

.... [2]

(d) Why are four hydrogen atoms needed for each carbon atom in the methane molecule?

....

.... [2]

(e) (i) What inert (noble) gas structure do the hydrogen atoms have?

.... [1]

(ii) What inert (noble) gas structure does the carbon atom have?

.... [1]

(iii) When atoms within a molecule form chemical bonds, they normally end up with eight electrons in their outer energy level. Why do the hydrogen atoms have only two?

.... [1]

[Total: 10]

5 Chemical calculations

Use the values of A_r which follow to answer the questions below.

H = 1; C = 12; N = 14; O = 16; Na = 23; Mg = 24; Al = 27; S = 32;
Cl = 35.5; Ca = 40; Fe = 56; Cu = 63.5

One mole of any gas at r.t.p. occupies a volume of 24 dm³.

1 (a) Calculate the relative molecular mass of each of the following compounds.

   (i) C_2H_5OH ....

   (ii) $CH_3COOCH_2CH_3$ ....

   (iii) CH_3CH_2COOH ....

   (iv) $CH_3CH=CH_2$ .... (4 marks)

(b) Calculate the relative formula mass of each of the following compounds.

   (i) Na_2CO_3 ....

   (ii) $Ca(OH)_2$ ....

   (iii) $(NH_4)_2SO_4$ ....

   (iv) Fe_2O_3 .... (4 marks)

2 (a) Calculate the number of moles of the element in:

   (i) 54 g of aluminium ....

   ....

   (ii) 0.4 g of calcium ....

   ....

   (iii) 18 g of iron. ....

   .... (3 marks)

(b) Calculate the number of moles of the compound in:

   (i) 51 g of aluminium oxide (Al_2O_3) ....

   ....

   (ii) 116 g of butane (C_4H_{10}) ....

   ....

   (iii) 480 g of iron(III) oxide (Fe_2O_3). ....

   .... (3 marks)

3 Calculate the mass of:

(a) 2 moles of calcium carbonate ....

(b) 0.5 mole of magnesium oxide ....

(c) 0.125 mole of aluminium oxide ....

(d) 10 moles of sodium chloride ....

(e) 0.25 mole of water ....

(f) 2.5 moles of sodium hydroxide. .... **(6 marks)**

4 (a) Calculate the empirical formulae of the compounds with the following compositions by mass.

(i) 24.0 g of calcium and 5.6 g of nitrogen

....

....

....

....

....(2 marks)

(ii) 50.8 g of copper and 6.4 g of oxygen

....

....

....

....

.... (2 marks)

(iii) 5.8 g of aluminium and 23.3 g of chlorine

....

....

....

....

.... (2 marks)

(iv) 2.18 g of carbon, 0.36 g of hydrogen and 1.46 g of oxygen

....

....

....

....

.... (2 marks)

(b) Calculate the empirical formulae of the compounds with the following percentage compositions by mass.
  (i) 92.3% carbon and 7.7% hydrogen

  ....

  ....

  ....

  .... (2 marks)

  (ii) 60.0% magnesium and 40.0% oxygen

  ....

  ....

  ....

  .... (2 marks)

  (iii) an oxide of iron that contains 70% of iron

  ....

  ....

  ....

  .... (2 marks)

  (iv) 27.4% sodium, 1.2% hydrogen, 14.3% carbon and 57.1% oxygen

  ....

  ....

  ....

  .... (2 marks)

(c) The empirical formula of a compound is CH_2. It has a relative molecular mass of 56. What is the molecular formula of the compound?

  ....

  .... (2 marks)

(d) The empirical formula of a compound is C_2H_4O. It has a relative molecular mass of 88. What is the molecular formula of the compound?

  ....

  .... (2 marks)

5 (a) Calculate the number of moles of solute in each of the following solutions.

  (i) 0.5 dm³ of 0.25 mol dm⁻³ NaOH

  ....

  ....

  (ii) 100 cm³ of 0.5 mol dm⁻³ NaCl

  ....

  ....

  (iii) 250 cm³ of 0.75 mol dm⁻³ HCl

  ....

  ....

  (iv) 500 cm³ of 1.5 mol dm⁻³ NaNO₃

  ....

  .... **(4 marks)**

(b) Calculate the concentration (in mol dm⁻³) of each of the following solutions.

  (i) 0.5 mole of sodium hydroxide in 500 cm³

  ....

  ....

  (ii) 0.25 mole of copper(II) sulfate in 250 cm³

  ....

  ....

  (iii) 0.1 mole of sodium carbonate in 250 cm³

  ....

  ....

  (iv) 0.3 mole of nitric acid in 100 cm³

  ....

  .... **(8 marks)**

(c) (i) How many grams of sodium hydroxide would be needed to make 250 cm³ of solution of concentration 0.1 mol dm⁻³?

  ....

  .... **(2 marks)**

  (ii) How many grams of sodium nitrate would be needed to make 500 cm³ of solution of concentration 0.25 mol dm⁻³?

  ....

  .... **(2 marks)**

6 To find out the concentration of a solution of hydrochloric acid, a student carried out a titration. She found that 18.95 cm³ of the hydrochloric acid was needed to neutralise 25 cm³ of a 0.1 mol dm⁻³ sodium carbonate solution.

(a) Write a balanced chemical equation for the reaction between hydrochloric acid and sodium carbonate.

.... (3 marks)

(b) Describe how the titration procedure was carried out.

....

....

....

.... (5 marks)

(c) Use the information given to find the concentration of the hydrochloric acid solution.

....

....

.... (3 marks)

7 When nitrogen gas (N_2) and oxygen gas (O_2) react together, they form an oxide of nitrogen. When 1.40 g of nitrogen gas reacted with oxygen gas, 4.60 g of the nitrogen oxide was formed.

(a) Use the information given to write a balanced chemical equation for the reaction taking place.

....

....

....

.... (4 marks)

(b) 0.24 g of magnesium metal reacts completely with some hydrochloric acid solution of concentration 1.0 mol dm⁻³.

(i) Write a balanced chemical equation for the reaction.

.... (3 marks)

(ii) How many moles of magnesium are used in the experiment?

.... (2 marks)

(iii) What volume of hydrochloric acid would be needed to react with the magnesium metal?

....

.... (2 marks)

(iv) What mass of magnesium chloride would be made in the experiment?

....

.... (2 marks)

(v) What volume of hydrogen gas would be produced?

....

.... (2 marks)

8 A student carried out a reaction between iron and hydrochloric acid to make some iron(II) chloride crystals. She started with 5.6 g of iron and used an excess of hydrochloric acid.

(a) (i) Write a balanced chemical equation for the reaction.

.... (3 marks)

(ii) How many moles of iron did she start off with?

.... (1 mark)

(iii) What mass of iron(II) chloride could she have expected to obtain from this reaction?

....

.... (2 marks)

(iv) She actually obtained 9.17 g of the iron(II) chloride. What was her percentage yield?

.... (2 marks)

(b) Iron is extracted from its ore haematite (Fe_2O_3) in the blast furnace. The reaction which produces the iron is:

$Fe_2O_3(s) + 3CO(g) \rightarrow 2Fe(s) + 3CO_2(g)$

100 tonnes of haematite gave 7 tonnes of iron. Calculate the percentage yield of the process.

....

....

....

.... (4 marks)

Stretch and challenge

9 When sodium chloride reacts with concentrated sulfuric acid, hydrogen chloride gas (HCl) is one of the products.

$H_2SO_4(l) + NaCl(s) \rightarrow NaHSO_4(s) + HCl(g)$

If hydrogen chloride gas is dissolved in water, a solution of hydrochloric acid is formed. What would be the concentration of the hydrochloric acid obtained if the reaction was carried out using 11.7 g of sodium chloride, and the hydrogen chloride gas was dissolved in 250 cm³ of water?

....

....

....

.... (4 marks)

10 A student carried out a titration between sulfuric acid and potassium carbonate solution to find out the concentration of the acid. She found that 23.55 cm³ of the sulfuric acid was needed to neutralise 25 cm³ of a 0.05 mol dm⁻³ potassium carbonate solution.

(a) Write a balanced chemical equation for the reaction.

.... (3 marks)

(b) (i) How many moles of potassium carbonate solution were used in the experiment?

.... (2 marks)

(ii) How many moles of sulfuric acid would this number of moles of potassium carbonate react with?

.... (1 mark)

(c) Calculate the concentration of the sulfuric acid used in the titration.

....

.... (2 marks)

■ *Exam focus*

1 (a) Copper(II) oxide can be reduced to copper by passing hydrogen gas over the oxide.

   $CuO(s) + H_2(g) \rightarrow Cu(s) + H_2O(g)$

   A student started the experiment with 8 g of copper(II) oxide and passed hydrogen gas over the heated oxide to produce copper metal.

   (i) What volume of hydrogen gas would be needed to react with all the copper(II) oxide?

   ....

   ....

   ....

   .... [3]

   (ii) What mass of copper metal could be obtained from this reaction?

   ....

   .... [2]

   (iii) The student obtained 5.8 g of copper. What was his percentage yield?

   .... [2]

(b) The hydrocarbon propane (C_3H_8) undergoes complete combustion as shown by the equation below.

   $C_3H_8(g) + 5O_2(g) \rightarrow 3CO_2(g) + 4H_2O(g)$

   (i) What volume of oxygen gas would be needed to react completely with 10 dm³ of propane gas?

   ....

   ....

   .... [3]

   (ii) What would be the total volume of gases produced from the reaction of propane with 10 dm³ of oxygen?

   ....

   ....

   .... [3]

   [Total: 13]

2 This question is about a titration involving the neutralisation reaction of 25 cm³ of dilute sodium hydroxide with dilute sulfuric acid.

The initial concentration of the dilute sodium hydroxide was 0.25 mol dm⁻³. The solution in the burette was dilute sulfuric acid. The indicator used was phenolphthalein. The table shows the titration results.

	Rough	1	2	3
Final burette reading/cm³	21.75	28.25	22.35	27.30
Initial burette reading/cm³	0.00	6.00	0.00	5.00
Volume of sulfuric acid used/cm³				

(a) Complete the table by calculating the volume of dilute sulfuric acid used in each titration. [1]

(b) From the three most accurate results, calculate the average volume of sulfuric acid used.

....

.... [2]

(c) Write a balanced chemical equation for the reaction.

.... [3]

(d) From the information given, calculate the number of moles of sodium hydroxide in 25 cm³ of solution.

....

.... [2]

(e) How many moles of sulfuric acid were neutralised?

.... [1]

(f) Calculate the concentration of the dilute sulfuric acid.

....

.... [2]

[Total: 11]

6 Electrolysis and its uses

1 The diagram below shows an electrolytic cell that could be used to study the electrolysis of molten lead(II) bromide. The labels have been replaced with numbers.

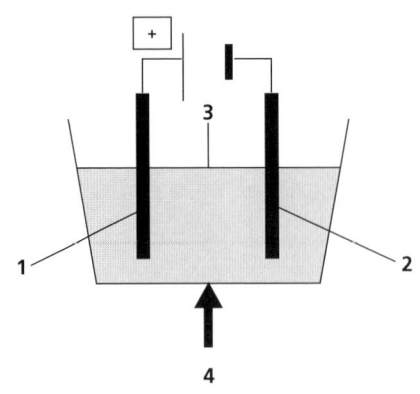

(a) For each number, write down the correct label from the list below. (4 marks)

| anode | cathode | electrolyte | heat |

1 ....

2 ....

3 ....

4 ....

(b) Define the term *electrolysis*.

.... (2 marks)

(c) Explain the meaning of each of the following terms.

(i) anode .... (1 mark)

(ii) cathode .... (1 mark)

(iii) electrolyte .... (2 marks)

(d) The anode and cathode are referred to as *electrodes*. What do you understand by that term?

....

.... (2 marks)

(e) What substance would the anode and cathode be made from?

.... (1 mark)

(f) In the electrolysis of lead(II) bromide, explain why the substance has to be *molten* for electrolysis to happen.

....

.... (2 marks)

2 Explain the meaning of each term shown in italics in the following paragraph.

Electrolysis is often defined as the *decomposition* of a substance, called the electrolyte, caused by the passage of an electric current. For this process to take place, the substance has to be either in *aqueous solution* or molten. During electrolysis, the *anions* are attracted to the positively charged *electrode* whilst the *cations* are attracted to the negatively charged electrode. The electrodes are usually *inert*. *Oxidation* takes place at the anode. *Reduction* takes place at the cathode.

(a) decomposition ....

.... (2 marks)

(b) aqueous solution ....

.... (2 marks)

(c) anions ....

.... (2 marks)

(d) cations ....

.... (2 marks)

(e) inert ....

.... (2 marks)

(f) oxidation ....

.... (2 marks)

(g) reduction ....

.... (2 marks)

3 The equations below show either oxidation or reduction taking place at the electrodes during an electrolysis process. For each equation, write down whether it is oxidation or reduction, and at which electrode the reaction takes place.

(a) $2H^+ + 2e^- \rightarrow H_2$

.... (2 marks)

(b) $2Cl^- \rightarrow Cl_2 + 2e^-$

.... (2 marks)

(c) $2O^{2-} \rightarrow O_2 + 4e^-$

.... (2 marks)

(d) $K^+ + e^- \rightarrow K$

.... (2 marks)

(e) $Mg^{2+} + 2e^- \rightarrow Mg$

.... (2 marks)

(f) $2F^- \rightarrow F_2 + 2e^-$

.... (2 marks)

4 Balance the following ionic equations for processes that take place at the electrodes during electrolysis.

(a) Na⁺ + ... → Na (1 mark)

(b) .... Br⁻ → .... + 2e⁻ (2 marks)

(c) Ca²⁺ + ... → .... (2 marks)

(d) .... + ... → Cu (2 marks)

(e) .... I⁻ → .... + ... (3 marks)

(f) .... OH⁻ → .... H₂O + ... + ... e⁻ (4 marks)

5 For each of the following statements about electrolysis, write either 'true' or 'false'.

(a) Covalent substances generally undergo electrolysis. .... (1 mark)

(b) Molten salts can conduct electricity because their ions are free to move.

.... (1 mark)

(c) During electrolysis, if oxygen gas is produced it comes off at the anode.

.... (1 mark)

(d) Inert electrodes are generally made from carbon or platinum.

.... (1 mark)

(e) When solid copper chloride is electrolysed, copper is produced at the cathode. .... (1 mark)

(f) During electrolysis, if hydrogen gas is produced it comes off at the cathode. .... (1 mark)

6 The table below shows the results of testing a number of solid and liquid substances to see if they conducted an electric current. The electrodes used were made from platinum in each case.

Substance	Physical state	Conductivity	Products
T	Liquid	Yes	Hydrogen and chlorine
U	Liquid	Yes	Silvery metal and green vapour
V	Liquid	No	None
W	Liquid	Yes	Hydrogen and oxygen
X	Liquid	Yes	None
Y	Solid	Yes	None
Z	Liquid	Yes	Pink-brown metal and oxygen

(a) Which of these substances, T to Z, are electrolytes? .... (4 marks)

(b) Which of these substances, T to Z, may be metals? .... (2 marks)

(c) Which of these substances, T to Z, may be sodium chloride? .... (1 mark)

(d) Which of these substances, T to Z, may be mercury? .... (1 mark)

(e) Which of these substances, **T** to **Z**, may be sugar solution? .... (1 mark)

(f) Give the name of a substance that **W** may be.

.... (1 mark)

(g) Give the name of a substance that **Z** may be.

.... (1 mark)

7 Complete the table below about a series of electrolysis experiments.

Substance	Material of electrodes	Substance formed at the cathode	Substance formed at the anode
Molten lead(II) chloride	Carbon		
	Platinum	Hydrogen	Oxygen
Molten calcium bromide			
		Sodium	Chlorine
Copper(II) sulfate solution	Copper		

(10 marks)

8 Explain the following.

(a) In the purification of copper by electrolysis, it is essential that a little dilute sulfuric acid is added to the electrolyte.

....

.... (1 mark)

(b) In the electrolysis of concentrated sodium chloride solution, it is necessary to keep the chlorine gas and sodium hydroxide separated.

....

.... (2 marks)

(c) In the extraction of aluminium from aluminium oxide, the anodes are replaced regularly.

....

.... (2 marks)

(d) In any electroplating process, it is necessary to degrease the metal to be plated before the process is started.

....

.... (2 marks)

Stretch and challenge

9 The diagram below shows an electrolysis cell.

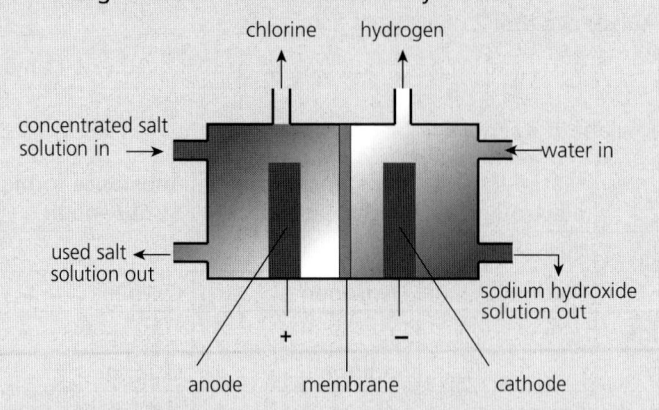

(a) Name the materials used to make:
   (i) the anode ....
   (ii) the cathode. ....
(b) (i) Hydrogen is produced at the cathode. Balance the following electrode equation for this process.

   $H^+(aq) + e^- \rightarrow H_2(g)$

   .... (2 marks)

   (ii) Chlorine is produced at the anode. Balance the following electrode equation for this process.

   $Cl^-(aq) \rightarrow Cl_2 + e^-$

   .... (2 marks)

   (iii) Give two large-scale uses for hydrogen and for chlorine.

   .... (4 marks)

(c) The overall chemical equation which represents what is happening in the electrolysis cell shown above is:

   $2NaCl(aq) + 2H_2O(l) \rightarrow 2NaOH(aq) + Cl_2(g) + H_2(g)$

   If 234 g of sodium chloride was electrolysed, calculate the mass of each of the following substances that would be formed. (A_r values: H = 1; O = 16; Na = 23; Cl = 35.5)
   (i) sodium hydroxide

   .... (2 marks)

   (ii) chlorine

   .... (2 marks)

   (iii) hydrogen

   .... (2 marks)

   (iv) Give two large-scale uses for sodium hydroxide.

   .... (2 marks)

Stretch and challenge

10 On the industrial scale, pure zinc is obtained by electrolysis of acidified zinc sulfate solution using zinc cathodes and lead anodes.

(a) (i) Write a balanced ionic equation for the process that is involved in the depositing of zinc at the cathode.

.... (3 marks)

(ii) Give two uses for pure zinc.

.... (2 marks)

(b) (i) What substance do you think is produced at the lead anodes?

.... (1 mark)

(ii) Write a balanced ionic equation for the process that is involved in the production of the substance you have named in your answer to part **(i)**.

.... (3 marks)

(iii) Give two uses for the substance you have named in your answer to part **(i)**.

.... (2 marks)

(c) The voltages are adjusted to ensure that a dangerously explosive gas is not produced. What is the name of this gas?

.... (1 mark)

(d) During the electrolysis process, zinc sulfate is passed continuously through the electrolysis tanks containing the electrodes. Why does the zinc sulfate have to be passed continuously through the tanks?

....

.... (2 marks)

■ *Exam focus*

1 Aluminium is an extremely useful metal. It is the most abundant metallic element found in the Earth's crust. It is extracted by electrolysis from its ore, bauxite. Pure aluminium oxide is separated chemically from bauxite and dissolved in molten cryolite. It is then electrolysed in a steel cell lined with carbon.

(a) Why is aluminium extracted from its oxide by electrolysis rather than by using a chemical reducing agent such as the element carbon?

....

.... [2]

(b) The electrolysis cell operates at about 1000 °C. This is well below the melting point of aluminium oxide, which is 2070 °C. How is the molten state maintained so that electrolysis can take place?

....

.... [2]

(c) (i) At which electrode is the aluminium produced? .... [1]
   (ii) Balance the following equation for the depositing of aluminium.

   $Al^{3+} + e^- \rightarrow Al$

   .... [1]

(d) (i) Oxygen gas is produced at the other electrode. What is this electrode made from?

   .... [1]

   (ii) Balance the following equation for the production of oxygen gas at this electrode.

   $O^{2-} \rightarrow O_2 + e^-$

   .... [2]

(e) (i) What further chemical reaction takes place at the electrode where oxygen is produced?

   .... [2]

   (ii) Write a balanced chemical equation for this reaction.

   .... [2]

(f) Why are aluminium smelters situated in hilly or mountainous areas?

.... [2]

(g) Large amounts of aluminium are recycled. Suggest two advantages of doing this.

....

.... [2]

[Total: 17]

2. Food cans are usually made from mild steel with a thin layer of tin deposited on its surface by electrolysis. A simplified diagram of the electroplating process is shown below.

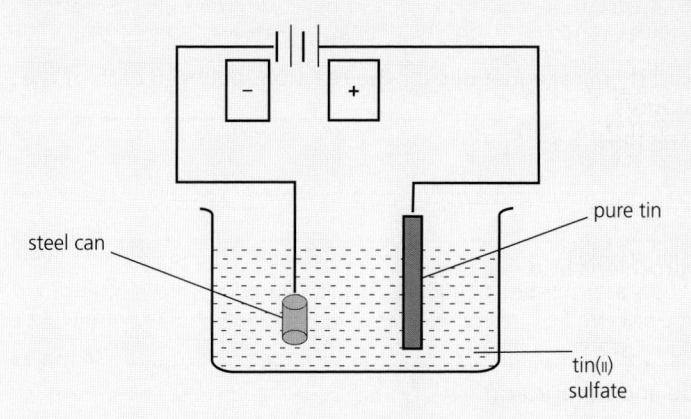

(a) (i) How does the mass of the cathode change during the process?

.... [1]

(ii) Why does the mass of the cathode change?

.... [1]

(b) (i) What charge do the tin ions in the tin(II) sulfate solution carry?

.... [1]

(ii) How did you decide on your answer to part **(i)**?

.... [1]

(c) (i) Does the concentration of the tin(II) sulfate solution differ at the end of the process compared to the beginning?

.... [1]

(ii) Explain your answer to part **(i)**.

.... [2]

(d) (i) Write a balanced equation for the electrode process that takes place at the cathode for the depositing of tin.

.... [3]

(ii) Write a balanced equation for the electrode process that takes place at the anode.

.... [3]

(e) Steel used to be plated by dipping it into molten tin. Why has this method been replaced by electroplating?

.... [2]

(f) Suggest a reason why food cans are made from mild steel electroplated with tin rather than from mild steel alone.

.... [1]

[Total: 16]

7 Acids, bases and salts

1. Write word and balanced chemical equations for the reactions between each of the following pairs of substances.

   (a) sodium carbonate and nitric acid

   ....

   .... (4 marks)

   (b) magnesium and hydrochloric acid

   ....

   .... (4 marks)

   (c) potassium hydroxide and sulfuric acid

   ....

   .... (4 marks)

   (d) copper(II) oxide and nitric acid

   ....

   .... (4 marks)

2. Complete the table below, which is about the different methods of preparing soluble and insoluble salts.

Substances used to make the salt		Salt prepared	Other products
Calcium oxide	Hydrochloric acid		
	Sulfuric acid	Sodium sulfate	Water
Potassium carbonate		Potassium nitrate	Water and carbon dioxide
	Hydrochloric acid	Zinc chloride	Hydrogen
Lead nitrate	Sodium chloride		Sodium nitrate
Barium chloride	Potassium sulfate		

(8 marks)

3 The diagram below shows some reactions of iron.

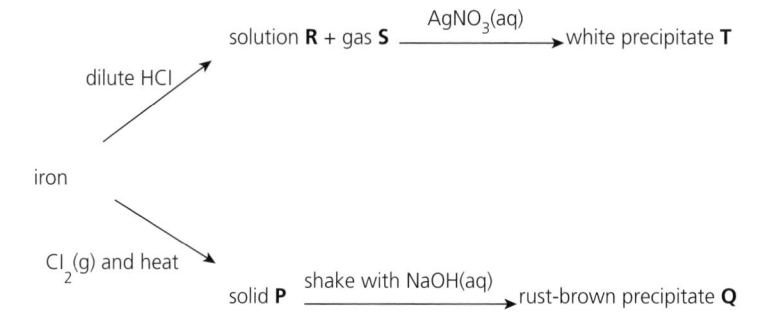

```
                              AgNO₃(aq)
           solution R + gas S ──────────→ white precipitate T
          ↗
   dilute HCl
          ↗
  iron
          ↘
   Cl₂(g) and heat
          ↘                shake with NaOH(aq)
                  solid P ─────────────────→ rust-brown precipitate Q
```

Name and give the formulae of the substances **P** to **T** shown in the diagram.

(a) solid **P** .... (2 marks)

(b) rust-brown precipitate **Q** .... (2 marks)

(c) solution **R** .... (2 marks)

(d) gas **S** .... (2 marks)

(e) white precipitate **T** .... (2 marks)

4 Explain how you would identify the presence, in solution, of each of the following ions.

(a) chloride, bromide and iodide ions

   (i) Cl⁻ ....

   .... (2 marks)

   (ii) Br⁻ ....

   .... (2 marks)

   (iii) I⁻ ....

   .... (2 marks)

(b) carbonate ions ....

   .... (2 marks)

(c) sulfate ions ....

   .... (2 marks)

(d) iron(II) and iron(III) ions

   (i) Fe²⁺ ....

   .... (2 marks)

   (ii) Fe³⁺ ....

   .... (2 marks)

5 (a) Use the data given in the table below to plot a solubility curve for potassium nitrate.

Temperature/°C	10	20	30	40	50	60
Solubility/g per 100 g of water	20	31	45	60	82	104

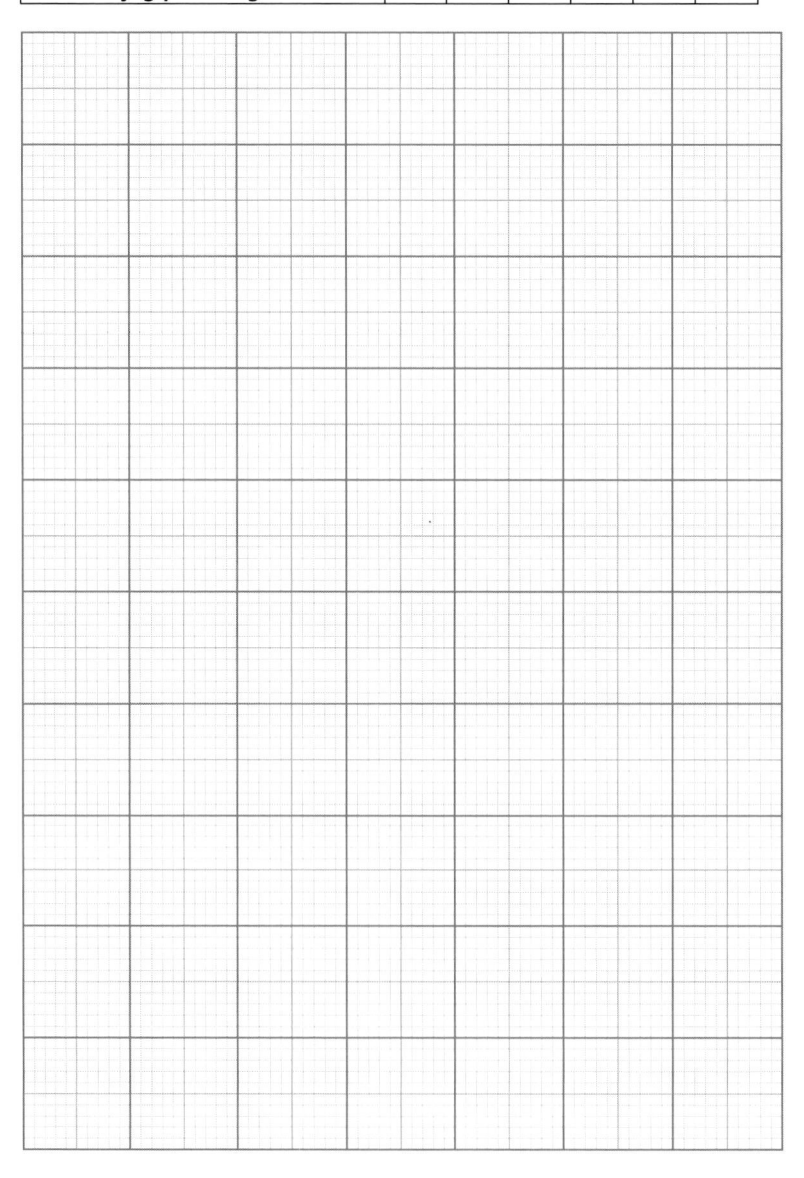

(4 marks)

Use your solubility curve from part **(a)** to answer the following questions.

(b) What is the solubility of potassium nitrate at:

(i) 25 °C? ....

(ii) 43 °C? ....

(iii) 52 °C? .... (3 marks)

(c) At what temperature does potassium nitrate have a solubility of:

(i) 50 g per 100 g of water? ....

(ii) 75 g per 100 g of water? ....

(iii) 95 g per 100 g of water? .... (3 marks)

(d) (i) What mass of potassium nitrate would dissolve in 25 cm³ of water at 35 °C?

....

.... (2 marks)

(ii) What mass of potassium nitrate would dissolve in 40 cm³ of water at 55 °C?

....

.... (2 marks)

(e) 100 cm³ of a saturated solution of potassium nitrate is cooled from 47 °C to 23 °C. Calculate the amount of potassium nitrate that would crystallise out of solution. (Assume that the density of water is 1 g/cm³.)

....

.... (3 marks)

6 (a) Write down the names of two chemical solutions that could be added together to form each of the following insoluble salts by a precipitation reaction.

(i) silver chloride

.... (2 marks)

(ii) barium sulfate

.... (2 marks)

(iii) calcium carbonate

.... (2 marks)

(b) Give full experimental details to explain how you could prepare a sample of the yellow insoluble salt lead(II) iodide. In your account, you should name the reactants and give a balanced *ionic* equation, with state symbols, for the reaction you would carry out.

....

....

....

.... (8 marks)

7 (a) What is the characteristic feature of an acid?

.... (2 marks)

(b) Describe what is meant by each of the following terms.

  (i) a weak acid ....

  ....

  (ii) a strong acid ....

  .... (4 marks)

(c) Write equations to show:

  (i) the ionisation of hydrochloric acid

  .... (2 marks)

  (ii) the ionisation of ethanoic acid.

  .... (2 marks)

(d) Explain the difference between the terms *strong* and *weak acids* compared with *concentrated* and *dilute acids*.

....

....

....

.... (4 marks)

8 The following passage describes the preparation of the salt potassium chloride. Read the passage and answer the questions that follow.

Put 25 cm³ of hydrochloric acid into a beaker. Add powdered sodium carbonate a small amount at a time until the reaction stops. Filter, and then evaporate the solution carefully on a water bath to remove some of the water. Leave the concentrated solution to crystallise.

(a) What is seen as the sodium carbonate is added to the hydrochloric acid?

.... (1 mark)

(b) How do you know when all of the acid has been used up?

.... (1 mark)

(c) What is removed by filtering?

.... (1 mark)

(d) Why is it important not to evaporate all the water away?

.... (1 mark)

(e) There are three products in this reaction. Water is one of them. Write a word equation for the reaction.

.... (2 marks)

(f) Write a balanced symbol equation for the reaction.

.... (3 marks)

Stretch and challenge

9 A chemistry teacher arrived in the laboratory to find that the labels had fallen off the bottles containing some solutions. He knew from the labels that the bottles contained **hydrochloric acid, iron(II) sulfate, sodium bromide, potassium carbonate** and **potassium iodide**, but he did not know which was which.

Using simple test-tube reactions, explain how he could identify which chemical was in each bottle. You should give a clear account of the steps you would carry out.

....
....
....
....
....
....
....
....
....
....
....
.... **(7 marks)**

Exam focus

1 (a) A reaction is carried out to prepare a sample of sodium sulfate crystals starting from dilute sodium hydroxide and dilute sulfuric acid. The reaction is carried out using a titration. Explain clearly how you would prepare the sodium sulfate crystals.

....

....

....

....

....

....

.... [7]

(b) Write a balanced chemical equation for the reaction between sodium hydroxide and sulfuric acid.

.... [3]

[Total: 10]

2 (a) Complete the following paragraph.

Acids dissolve in water to produce .... ions, which can be written as .... Alkalis are soluble .... They dissolve in water to produce .... ions, which can be written as .... Acids and alkalis react together to produce solutions with a pH of 7; these are called .... reactions. [6]

(b) Write an ionic equation for the neutralisation reaction which takes place when an acid reacts with an alkali.

.... [3]

(c) In a reaction between potassium carbonate and hydrochloric acid to produce potassium chloride crystals, the following method was used.
25 cm^3 of hydrochloric acid was placed in a beaker. Solid potassium carbonate was added to the acid and effervescence was seen. The mixture was stirred and potassium carbonate was added until some remained at the bottom of the beaker. The mixture was then filtered and the filtrate collected in an evaporating basin. The filtrate was heated until about one half had evaporated and crystals were starting to form. The solution which remained was allowed to cool, and crystals formed.

(i) Write a balanced chemical equation for the reaction.

.... [3]

(ii) Why was potassium carbonate added until some remained at the bottom of the beaker?

.... [1]

(iii) What was the name of the filtrate? .... [1]

(iv) What name is given to a solution which has crystals starting to form from it? .... [1]

[Total: 15]

8 Inorganic carbon chemistry

1. For each of the following statements, write either 'true' or 'false'.

    (a) Chalk is not a form of calcium carbonate. .... (1 mark)

    (b) Marble is a sedimentary rock. .... (1 mark)

    (c) When limestone is subjected to high temperatures and pressure, marble is formed. .... (1 mark)

    (d) Calcium carbonate, $CaCO_3$, contains three elements and has a total of four atoms that make up the formula. .... (1 mark)

    (e) Limestone was formed in a marine environment. .... (1 mark)

    (f) Chalk is a soft natural form of calcium carbonate. .... (1 mark)

2. Limestone is a very important raw material in a number of industries.

    (a) What do you understand by the term *raw material*?

    .... (2 marks)

    (b) Name three important uses for limestone.

    ....

    .... (3 marks)

    (c) Limestone is obtained by open-cast mining. What are the advantages and disadvantages to the local community of an open-cast limestone mine in their area?

    ....

    ....

    ....

    .... (6 marks)

3. (a) (i) Calcium hydroxide, or slaked lime, is a cheap industrial alkali. Explain the meaning of the term *alkali*.

    ....

    .... (3 marks)

    (ii) Name two large-scale uses for calcium hydroxide.

    ....

    .... (2 marks)

    (b) (i) A weak solution of calcium hydroxide in water is called limewater. It is used to test for carbon dioxide gas. Explain what happens in this test, giving the chemical name and formula of the major substance produced during the test.

    ....

    .... (3 marks)

(ii) If carbon dioxide is passed through limewater continuously, a further change takes place. Describe what happens to the limewater solution and give an explanation of what is happening, along with the name and formula of the major product.

....

....

....

.... (4 marks)

(iii) If calcium hydroxide is mixed with sand, what useful building material is produced?

.... (1 mark)

4 (a) Explain how you could test for the presence of a carbonate such as calcium carbonate. In your explanation, give word and balanced chemical equations to help with your explanation.

....

....

....

....

.... (7 marks)

(b) Carbonates are generally quite useful substances. For example, sodium carbonate is a very important industrial chemical.

(i) Give the chemical formula of sodium carbonate. .... (1 mark)

(ii) Name three uses for this important carbonate.

....

.... (3 marks)

(c) (i) Almost all hydrogencarbonates are known only in solution. Why is this the case?

....

.... (1 mark)

(ii) Name two hydrogencarbonates that are found only in solution.

....

.... (2 marks)

(iii) Sodium hydrogencarbonate ($NaHCO_3$) is the most common solid hydrogencarbonate. It is found in indigestion remedies. Why is this substance put into these remedies?

....

.... (2 marks)

5 (a) Biologically, water is essential for the existence of all life on Earth. It is also extremely important in the manufacture of some bulk industrial chemicals. Name two important industrial chemicals that require water in their manufacture. Also give the chemical formulae of your chosen substances.

....

.... (4 marks)

(b) Water is also an excellent solvent and will dissolve a whole range of solutes.

(i) Explain what the terms *solvent* and *solute* mean.

....

....

....

.... (4 marks)

(ii) Which of the following substances would be classified as a solute with water as the solvent?

> iron   petrol   potassium nitrate
> sodium chloride   sugar

....

.... (3 marks)

(iii) Describe the effect on the solubility of a solute when the temperature of the solvent (for example water) is increased.

.... (1 mark)

(c) Water can be classified as *hard* or *soft*. What is the difference between these two types of water?

....

....

....

.... (4 marks)

6 In recent years, scientists have detected an increase in the amount of carbon dioxide in the atmosphere. Carbon dioxide is a *greenhouse gas* and has been linked to *global warming*.

(a) Explain the meaning of each of the following terms.

(i) greenhouse gas

....

.... (2 marks)

(ii) global warming

....

.... (2 marks)

(b) Describe the effect that global warming will have on the Earth over time.

....

....

....

.... (3 marks)

7 (a) Carbon dioxide is one of the gaseous oxides of carbon. Name and give the formula of the other oxide.

....

.... (2 marks)

(b) Carbon dioxide is the more important of the two oxides. Large amounts are produced annually worldwide. Give two large-scale uses for carbon dioxide.

....

....

.... (2 marks)

(c) Which common mixture is carbon dioxide is obtained from? .... (1 mark)

(d) The diagram below shows the bonding in carbon dioxide.

(i) What type of bonding is present in this substance? .... (1 mark)

(ii) Carbon dioxide contains two double bonds. Explain the term *double bond* with reference to carbon dioxide.

....

....

.... (2 marks)

8 (a) Draw a labelled diagram of the apparatus that could be used to prepare a sample of carbon dioxide.

(6 marks)

(b) If you wanted a dry sample of the gas, how would you alter the apparatus to allow you to obtain this dry sample? Name any chemical substances you would use.

....

....

.... (4 marks)

(c) (i) Carbon dioxide will only allow very strongly burning substances, such as magnesium, to continue burning in it. Describe what you would see during this reaction.

....

.... (3 marks)

(ii) Balance the following chemical equation for this reaction.

.... Mg(s) + CO$_2$(g) → .... MgO(s) + C(s)   (2 marks)

(iii) Write the word equation for this reaction.

.... (1 mark)

(iv) This is a redox reaction. What do you understand by the term *redox reaction*?

....

.... (2 marks)

(v) Name and give the formulae of the reducing and oxidising agents in this reaction.

....

.... (4 marks)

Stretch and challenge

9 (a) Draw a simplified diagram of the carbon cycle. Include the following labels in your diagram:

> aerobic respiration
> combustion   photosynthesis

(6 marks)

(b) Explain the meaning of the three terms given in part (a).

....

....

....

....

....

....

....

....

....

....

....
.... (11 marks)

(c) Name and give the formula of the substance that carries the carbon around the carbon cycle.

.... (2 marks)

(d) Give the names of two other cycles that influence life on this planet.

.... (2 marks)

Stretch and challenge

10 (a) Burning fossil fuels makes a large contribution to the amount of carbon dioxide in the atmosphere.

    (i) Coal is a fossil fuel. What is a *fossil fuel*?

    ....

    .... (2 marks)

    (ii) Methane gas is also a fossil fuel. It usually occurs together with a further fossil fuel. Give the name of this other fossil fuel.

    .... (1 mark)

    (iii) The balanced chemical equation for burning methane in air is:

        $CH_4(g) + 2O_2(g) \rightarrow CO_2(g) + 2H_2O(l)$

    Calculate the mass of carbon dioxide produced when 32 g of methane is burned. (A_r values: H = 1; C = 12; O = 16)

    ....

    .... (2 marks)

    (iv) What volume of carbon dioxide would be produced when 32 g of methane is burned? (1 mole of gas occupies 24 dm³ at room temperature and pressure.)

    .... (2 marks)

(b) The formula of the major constituent of petrol is C_8H_{18}. Explain why you would expect petrol to produce more carbon dioxide than methane when it is burned inside car engines.

.... (1 mark)

■ *Exam focus*

1 Marble is a naturally occurring form of calcium carbonate, $CaCO_3$. When marble is heated, it decomposes in a chemical reaction to form quicklime by an endothermic reaction.

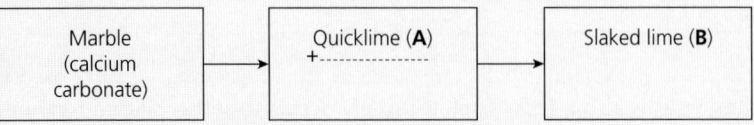

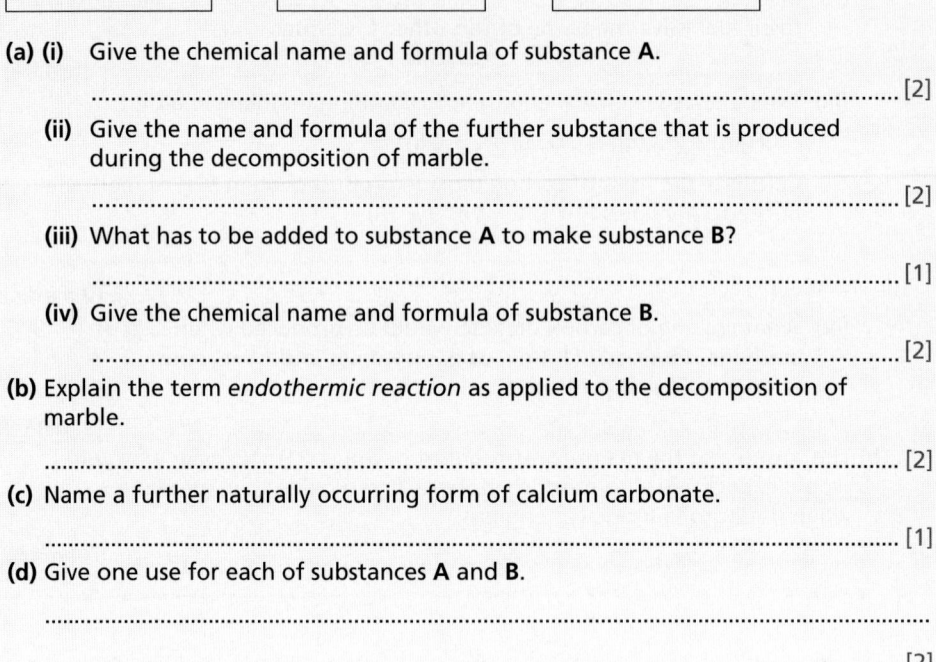

```
Marble              →    Quicklime (A)    →    Slaked lime (B)
(calcium                 + ----------
carbonate)
```

(a) (i) Give the chemical name and formula of substance **A**.

.... [2]

(ii) Give the name and formula of the further substance that is produced during the decomposition of marble.

.... [2]

(iii) What has to be added to substance **A** to make substance **B**?

.... [1]

(iv) Give the chemical name and formula of substance **B**.

.... [2]

(b) Explain the term *endothermic reaction* as applied to the decomposition of marble.

.... [2]

(c) Name a further naturally occurring form of calcium carbonate.

.... [1]

(d) Give one use for each of substances **A** and **B**.

....

.... [2]

[Total: 12]

2 Limestone is a very important industrial substance. It can be converted into quicklime in a kiln, a simplified diagram of which is shown below.

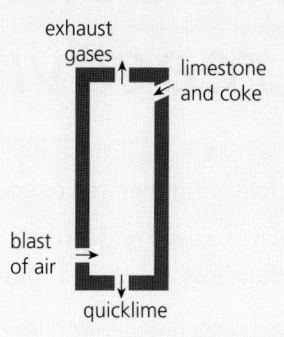

(a) How is the kiln heated?

.... [1]

(b) Why do you think hot air is blown through the kiln?

.... [2]

(c) The main reaction in the kiln involves the thermal decomposition of calcium carbonate. The balanced chemical equation is:

$CaCO_3(s) \rightarrow CaO(s) + CO_2(g)$

(i) What do you understand by the term *thermal decomposition*?

.... [2]

(ii) What mass of quicklime can be made from 100 tonnes of limestone?
(A_r values: C = 12; O = 16; Ca = 40)

....

.... [1]

(d) In addition to the above reaction in the kiln, there is a further reaction taking place in which carbon dioxide is produced. Write word and balanced chemical equations for this reaction.

....

.... [4]

(e) Modern kilns have been converted to be heated with a gaseous fuel. Name and give the formula of a possible gaseous fuel that could be used safely in this process.

.... [2]

[Total: 12]

9 Metal extraction and chemical reactivity

1. Complete and balance the following chemical equations.

   (a) .... + H_2SO_4(aq) → $MgSO_4$(aq) + H_2O(l) + ... (2 marks)

   (b) 2Ca(s) + O_2(g) → .... (1 mark)

   (c) Mg(s) + ... → $MgSO_4$(aq) + Zn(s) (1 mark)

   (d) .... + ... → 2MgO(s) (2 marks)

   (e) Zn(s) + 2 .... (aq) → .... + H_2(g) (2 marks)

2. The list below shows four metals in order of their chemical reactivity. Use it to answer the questions which follow.

   (most reactive)   zinc   iron   tin   copper   (least reactive)

   (a) (i) Write a chemical equation for the reaction which occurs when zinc powder (grey) is added to copper(II) sulfate solution (blue).

   ....
   .... (3 marks)

   (ii) What changes would you see when the zinc is added to copper(II) sulfate solution?

   ....
   .... (2 marks)

   (iii) Explain what happens to cause the changes you have described in your answer to part (ii).

   ....
   .... (2 marks)

   (b) Iron cans for containing food are usually coated with a layer of tin. Give two reasons why tin is a suitable metal for this purpose.

   ....
   .... (2 marks)

3 Write balanced chemical equations for the reactions between each of the following pairs of substances.

(a) lithium metal and water

.... (3 marks)

(b) zinc metal and hydrochloric acid

.... (3 marks)

(c) magnesium and copper(II) oxide

.... (3 marks)

(d) lead and silver nitrate solution

.... (3 marks)

(e) zinc metal and steam

.... (3 marks)

(f) magnesium metal and water

.... (3 marks)

4 This question concerns the extraction of iron from its ore haematite (Fe_2O_3) in the blast furnace.

(a) The coke that is added to the furnace fulfils two functions. What are they?

.... (2 marks)

(b) Why is limestone added as a raw material to the furnace?

.... (1 mark)

(c) Write chemical equations for each of the following processes, which occur in the blast furnace.

(i) the thermal decomposition of limestone

.... (3 marks)

(ii) the oxidation of carbon (coke)

.... (3 marks)

(iii) the formation of carbon monoxide

.... (3 marks)

(iv) the extraction of iron from the haematite

.... (3 marks)

(v) the formation of calcium silicate (slag)

.... (3 marks)

(d) What role does the carbon monoxide play in the extraction process?

.... (1 mark)

5 Magnesium metal is reacted with steam in a suitable apparatus. When the reaction occurs, a colourless gas **Y** is produced along with a white solid **Z**. Gas **Y** gives a squeaky 'pop' when mixed with air and ignited.

(a) Name gas **Y**. .... (1 mark)

(b) Write a balanced chemical equation for the reaction which occurs when gas **Y** is burned in air.

.... (3 marks)

(c) Name solid **Z**. .... (1 mark)

(d) Write a balanced chemical equation for the reaction which occurs when magnesium metal reacts with steam.

.... (3 marks)

(e) Name another metal which could safely be used to produce gas **Y** by reaction with steam. .... (1 mark)

6 A student carried out an experiment to find the order of reactivity of six different metals, labelled **A** to **F**. Small strips of each metal were placed into solutions of the nitrates of the other five metals. The student looked for a reaction occurring in each case.

(a) What would the student be looking for to see if a reaction was occurring?

.... (1 mark)

(b) If a reaction did occur, what type of reaction would the student be observing?

.... (1 mark)

(c) The table below shows a record of the student's results.

Metal	A nitrate	B nitrate	C nitrate	D nitrate	E nitrate	F nitrate
A	—	✓	✗	✗	✓	✓
B	✗	—	✗	✗	✓	✓
C	✓	✓	—	✓	✓	✓
D	✓	✓	✗	—	✓	✓
E	✗	✗	✗	✗	—	✗
F	✗	✗	✗	✗	✓	—

✓ reaction occurred   ✗ no reaction   — reaction not done

Put the metals **A** to **F** in order of their reactivity, with the least reactive metal first.

.... (3 marks)

7 The table below gives the compositions and properties of some different types of steel and cast iron.

Type of steel	Composition	Properties
Cast iron	96% Fe, 4% C	Very brittle, easily moulded, hard
Mild steel	99.5% Fe, 0.5% C	Easily worked, little brittleness, springy
Hard steel	99% Fe, 1% C	Tougher than mild steel, brittle
Stainless steel	74% Fe, 18% Cr, 8% Ni	Tough, does not rust
Tungsten steel	95% Fe, 5% W	Tough even at high temperatures

(a) (i) Which element that is present in steels and cast iron makes them brittle?
.... (1 mark)

(ii) How is the amount of the element you have named in your answer to part (i) reduced during the steel-making process?
.... (2 marks)

(b) Stainless steel is a mixture of three different metals. What name do we give to substances such as stainless steel?
.... (1 mark)

(c) Cars and ships made from steel often suffer from rusting. Stainless steel, however, does not rust. Why do we not make cars or ships out of stainless steel?
.... (2 marks)

(d) Complete the table below to give the properties required for the objects listed and the type of steel you would *choose* to make them out of.

Object	Properties	Steel
Chisel	Tough	Hard steel
Car body		
Axe		
Surgical knife		

(6 marks)

8 A student set up the experiment below to find out what conditions were needed for rusting to occur.

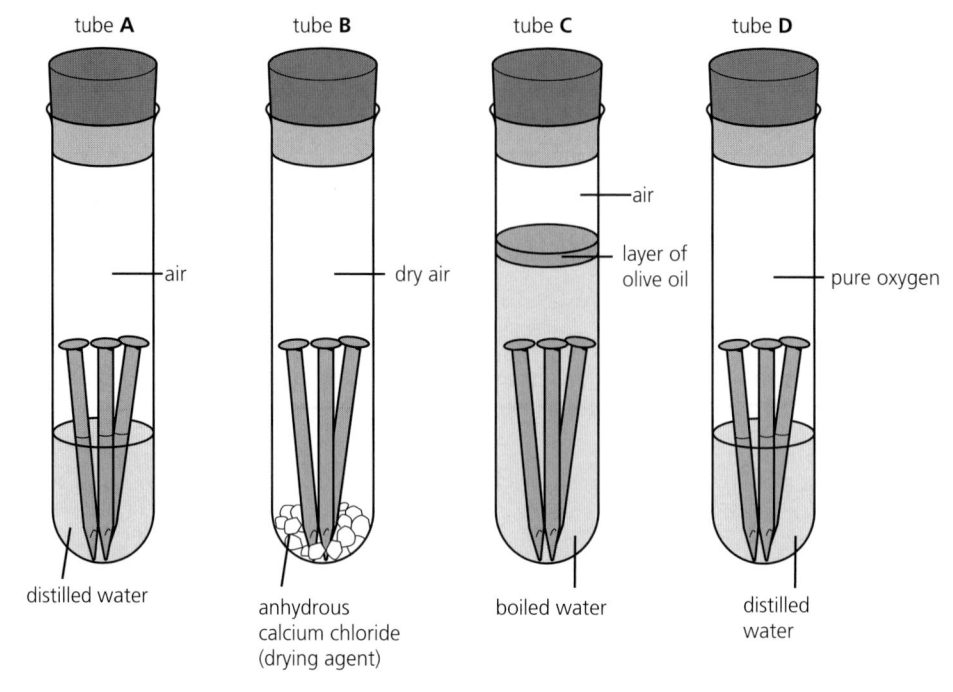

- tube **A**: air, distilled water
- tube **B**: dry air, anhydrous calcium chloride (drying agent)
- tube **C**: air, layer of olive oil, boiled water
- tube **D**: pure oxygen, distilled water

(a) What was the purpose of:

(i) the anhydrous calcium chloride in tube **B**?

.... (2 marks)

(ii) boiling the water in tube **C**?

.... (2 marks)

(iii) the layer of oil in tube **C**?

.... (2 marks)

(b) What conditions were present in each of the tubes? Put ticks in the table below to show if oxygen or water was present in each of the tubes.

Tube	Water	Oxygen
A		
B		
C		
D		

(4 marks)

(c) (i) In which tube(s) will the nails not rust? .... (2 marks)

(ii) Explain your answer to part **(i)**.

.... (2 marks)

(d) (i) In which tube will the nails rust the most?

....(1 mark)

(ii) Explain your answer to part **(i)**.

....(1 mark)

Stretch and challenge

9 When a mixture of copper(II) oxide and zinc metal reacts, a pink-brown solid is formed along with a yellow solid which changes colour to white when it gets cold.

(a) Write word and balanced chemical equations for the reaction which occurs.

....

.... (3 marks)

(b) Name the pink-brown solid that is formed in the reaction.

.... (1 mark)

(c) Name the solid which is yellow when hot and white when cold.

.... (1 mark)

(d) (i) Which of the reactants is being oxidised in this reaction?

.... (1 mark)

(ii) Explain why this reactant is being oxidised.

.... (1 mark)

(iii) What is happening to the other reactant when the reaction occurs?

.... (1 mark)

10 One way of extracting iron from iron(III) oxide is to react it with the more reactive metal aluminium. When 108 g of aluminium powder and iron(III) oxide react together, 180 g of iron is produced.

(a) Write a balanced chemical equation for the reaction.

.... (3 marks)

(b) Which reactant has been oxidised and which has been reduced during the reaction?

....

.... (2 marks)

(c) (i) What mass of iron could be produced from the reaction described?

....

....

.... (3 marks)

(ii) 180 g of iron was obtained from the reaction. What was the percentage yield?

.... (2 marks)

■ *Exam focus*

1 Look at the flow diagram shown below.

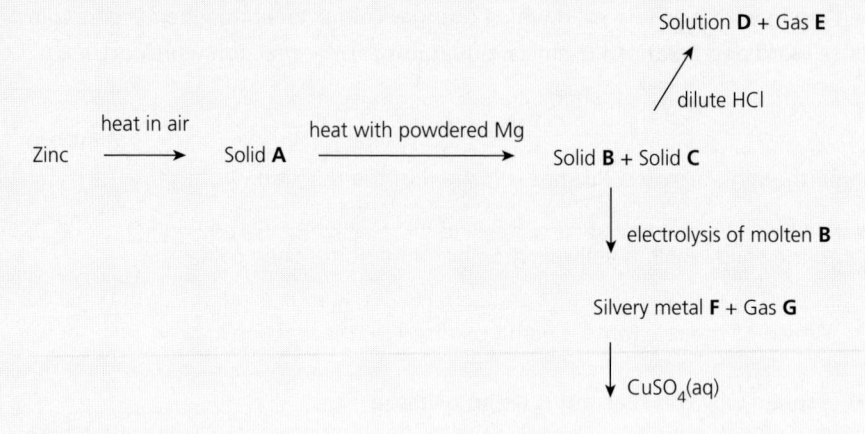

```
                                              Solution D + Gas E
                                                    ↑
                                                   / dilute HCl
              heat in air      heat with powdered Mg
    Zinc  ───────────→  Solid A ───────────────→  Solid B + Solid C
                                                       │
                                                       │ electrolysis of molten B
                                                       ↓
                                              Silvery metal F + Gas G
                                                       │
                                                       ↓ CuSO_4(aq)
                                              Brown-pink solid H + Solution I
```

(a) Name and give the formulae of substances **A** to **I**.

A .... [1]

B .... [1]

C .... [1]

D .... [1]

E .... [1]

F .... [1]

G .... [1]

H .... [1]

I .... [1]

(b) Write balanced chemical equations for the reactions in which:
   (i) solid **B** was formed

   .... [2]

   (ii) solution **D** and gas **E** were formed.

   .... [3]

(c) Write anode and cathode reactions for the processes which take place during the electrolysis of molten **B**.

   ....

   .... [6]

[Total: 20]

2 Use the reactivity series below to answer the questions which follow.

sodium
magnesium
zinc
iron
lead
hydrogen
copper
silver

increasing reactivity

(a) When lead(II) oxide reacts with iron, a redox reaction occurs.
  (i) Write a balanced chemical equation for the reaction.
  .... [2]
  (ii) What is a *redox reaction*?
  .... [2]
  (iii) Describe what is happening to the iron and the lead(II) oxide when the reaction occurs.
  ....
  .... [2]

(b) Magnesium reacts with hydrochloric acid to give a salt and hydrogen gas.
  (i) Write a balanced chemical equation for the reaction.
  .... [3]
  (ii) Copper metal does not react with acid. Explain why the reaction does not occur for copper but does occur for magnesium.
  .... [2]
  (iii) Name another metal that will not react with hydrochloric acid.
  .... [1]

(c) Zinc oxide is unusual in that it changes colour when it is heated. It is yellow when hot but white when cold. When zinc oxide reacts with magnesium metal, a white solid is obtained 10 minutes after the reaction has ended.
  (i) What is the white solid? .... [1]
  (ii) Write a balanced chemical equation for the reaction.
  .... [2]
  (iii) What would happen to the white solid obtained if it were heated?
  .... [1]

[Total: 16]

10 Atmosphere and oceans

1 The composition of the air has changed over millions of years. The table below shows the approximate composition of the Earth's atmosphere every 500 million years from when the Earth was formed, 4500 million years ago.

Millions of years ago	Approximate percentage of CO_2	Approximate percentage of O_2	Approximate percentage of gas A
4500	90	0	10
4000	40	0	30
3500	21	0.5	40
3000	15	1	55
2500	10	5	60
2000	7	10	70
1500	5	18	75
1000	2	20	76
500	1	21	77
0	0.04	21	78

(a) Draw a line graph to show how the approximate percentages of the three gases shown in the table have changed over time.

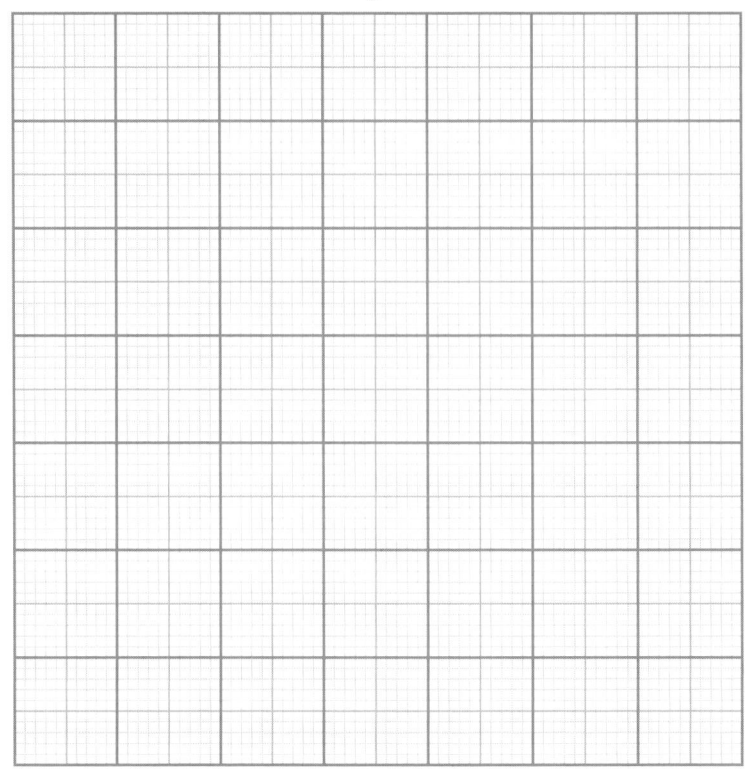

(7 marks)

(b) (i) What is the name of gas **A**? .... (1 mark)
   (ii) Explain the reasoning behind your answer to part **(i)**.
   ....
   .... (2 marks)

(c) On the time axis of your graph, mark the point where:
   (i) the first forms of bacteria appeared (1 mark)
   (ii) the first land plants appeared (1 mark)
   (iii) the oceans first appeared. (1 mark)

(d) Explain why the appearance of the first land plants caused a change in the amount of carbon dioxide in the atmosphere.
   ....
   .... (2 marks)

2 Oxygen gas was discovered independently by Joseph Priestley in Britain and by Carl Wilhelm Scheele in Sweden in 1773–74. However, the gas was named by the French scientist Antoine Lavoisier. It is now known to be the essential gas in the atmosphere for life to exist on this planet.

(a) It is now known that oxygen atoms have an atomic number of 8. What information does this give you about atoms of oxygen?
   ....
   .... (4 marks)

(b) Oxygen molecules that exist in the atmosphere are diatomic. Explain the meaning of the word *diatomic*.
   ....
   .... (2 marks)

(c) What type of bonding is present in oxygen molecules? .... (1 mark)

(d) Draw a bonding diagram of an oxygen molecule, showing the outermost energy levels only.

(3 marks)

(e) Give two uses for oxygen.
   .... (2 marks)

3 Nitrogen gas was discovered by Daniel Rutherford in 1772. It is now known to be a very important gas in the atmosphere. It is also an essential element necessary for the well being of animals and plants.

(a) It is now known that nitrogen atoms have an atomic number of 7. What information does this give you about atoms of nitrogen?

....

.... (4 marks)

(b) Nitrogen is a *diatomic gas and contains a triple bond between the nitrogen atoms*. With the aid of a bonding diagram, showing the outermost energy levels only, show that you understand the meaning of the phrase in italics.

....

.... (4 marks)

(c) (i) Which of the bonds found in the oxygen and nitrogen molecules is the strongest?

.... (1 mark)

(ii) Explain your answer to part (i).

....

....

.... (3 marks)

(d) Give two uses for nitrogen.

.... (2 marks)

4 Helium, neon and argon are noble gases found in the atmosphere.

(a) Which group in the periodic table do these elements belong to?

.... (1 mark)

(b) The atomic numbers and mass numbers of these elements are given below.

$^{4}_{2}He$ $^{20}_{10}Ne$ $^{40}_{18}Ar$

(i) What are the electronic structures of each of these elements?

.... (3 marks)

(ii) Why are these elements classified as inert gases?

.... (1 mark)

(iii) When elements combine by means of covalent bonds, what electronic structure do they try to achieve in their outer electron energy level?

.... (2 marks)

(c) Give a use for each of these gases based on their inert nature.

....

....

.... (3 marks)

5 Sea water contains about 35 g of dissolved substances per kilogram. The table below shows a typical analysis of some of the elemental ions present in sea water.

Ions	Concentration/ g per dm³ of sea water
Bromide	0.07
Calcium	0.4
Chloride	19.2
Magnesium	1.3
Potassium	0.4
Sodium	10.7
Other ions	2.3

(a) Calculate the mass of the dissolved elemental ions in 100 cm³ of sea water.

....

.... (2 marks)

(b) The concentrations of those ions found in sea water are much greater than those found in river water. Explain why this should be the case.

....

.... (2 marks)

(c) Write down the formulae of the following ions.

(i) bromide .... (1 mark)

(ii) chloride .... (1 mark)

(iii) potassium .... (1 mark)

(iv) calcium .... (1 mark)

(d) Using your answers to part **(c)**, write down the formulae of the following compounds.

(i) potassium chloride .... (1 mark)

(ii) calcium bromide .... (1 mark)

(e) (i) What do the data in the table indicate about the solubilities in water of calcium and sodium compounds?

.... (1 mark)

(ii) Explain your answer to part **(i)**.

....

.... (2 marks)

(f) Explain in terms of electron transfer what happens to sodium and potassium when they are converted into their respective ions.

....

....

.... (3 marks)

6 Water pollution has become a real problem. Water is such a good solvent that many substances will dissolve in it, including fertilisers.

(a) Explain how fertilisers get into rivers.

....

.... (2 marks)

(b) Give the names and formulae of the nitrogen-containing ions, from chemical fertilisers, that pollute water in rivers.

....

.... (4 marks)

(c) Name and give the formula of an artificial fertiliser that contains the ions you have named in your answer to part **(b)**.

.... (2 marks)

(d) (i) What materials are encouraged to grow in rivers by the presence of artificial fertilisers?

.... (2 marks)

(ii) What effect does the growth of these materials have on life in the river?

....

.... (2 marks)

7 Carbon monoxide is produced in quite large quantities by petrol and diesel engines. It is formed by the incomplete combustion of fuels in these engines.

(a) What do you understand by the term *incomplete combustion*?

....

.... (2 marks)

(b) Equations for the incomplete combustion of the main component in petrol are shown below.

octane + oxygen → carbon monoxide + water

.... $C_8H_{18}(l) + 17O_2(g) \rightarrow$ .... $CO(g)$ + ... H_2O

Balance the chemical equation above. (3 marks)

(c) (i) To remove the carbon monoxide from the exhaust fumes of a car, a catalytic converter is introduced into the exhaust system. What is the catalyst that this contains?

.... (1 mark)

(ii) In this catalytic converter, the carbon monoxide is converted into carbon dioxide by reaction with oxygen. Write a balanced chemical equation for this reaction.

.... (3 marks)

8 As well as the substances you would expect in pure dry air, other substances called pollutants are found in the atmosphere. These pollutants cause air pollution.

(a) Explain the meaning of the two sentences above, using specific examples where possible.

....

....

.... (3 marks)

(b) Sulfur dioxide is a pollutant. Major sources of this gas are heavy industry and power stations.

(i) From which three substances would sulfur dioxide be produced in these industries?

.... (3 marks)

(ii) The word and balanced chemical equations for the production of sulfur dioxide are given below.

sulfur + oxygen → sulfur dioxide

S(s) + O_2(g) → SO_2(g)

Calculate the mass of sulfur dioxide produced by 32 kg of sulfur. (A_r values: O = 16; S = 32)

....

.... (1 mark)

(iii) The sulfur dioxide dissolves in water in the atmosphere and produces an acid. This acid is then oxidised to a further acid. What are the names and formulae of the initial acid and the final acid produced on oxidation?

....

.... (4 marks)

(iv) What problems do the acids produced from sulfur dioxide in the air cause in the environment?

....

.... (3 marks)

(v) Units are being added to some power stations to prevent the emission of sulfur dioxide. What is the name given to these units?

.... (1 mark)

Stretch and challenge

9 Oxides of nitrogen are atmospheric pollutants. Motor vehicles are responsible for much of the pollution by these oxides that is found in the atmosphere in towns and cities.

(a) Nitrogen monoxide is formed by the reaction of nitrogen and oxygen inside the car engine. The word and symbol equations are given below.

nitrogen + oxygen → nitrogen monoxide

$N_2(g) + O_2(g) \rightarrow 2NO(g)$

(i) Calculate the volume of nitrogen monoxide produced at room temperature from 48 dm³ of nitrogen.

(1 mark)

(ii) As it exits the exhaust, the nitrogen monoxide produced in the car engine then reacts with oxygen from the air and forms the brown gas nitrogen(IV) oxide. This is an acidic gas. The word and symbol equations are given below.

nitrogen monoxide + oxygen → nitrogen(IV) oxide

.... $NO(g) + O_2(g) \rightarrow$ .... $NO_2(g)$

Balance the chemical equation above. (2 marks)

(iii) What attachment to a car would help to eliminate the problem of pollution by oxides of nitrogen?

.... (1 mark)

(b) When nitrogen(IV) oxide reacts with water from the atmosphere, an acid is produced along with some nitrogen monoxide.

(i) Name and give the formula of the acid produced.

.... (2 marks)

(ii) Write word and balanced chemical equations for the production of this acid.

....

.... (4 marks)

Stretch and challenge

10 The gases in the air can be separated by fractional distillation of liquid air. In this process, water vapour and carbon dioxide are removed from the air. The remaining gases in the air are then liquefied and separated by fractional distillation. The table below shows these gases, along with their boiling points.

Gas	Boiling point/°C
Argon	−186
Helium	−269
Krypton	−157
Neon	−246
Nitrogen	−196
Oxygen	−183
Xenon	−108

(a) How are solid particles removed from the air before the carbon dioxide and any water vapour are removed? .... **(1 mark)**

(b) To what temperature is the air cooled to remove the carbon dioxide and water vapour?
.... **(1 mark)**

(c) Before distilling the air, it is cooled to below −200 °C at high pressure.
  (i) Why is it necessary to remove the carbon dioxide and water vapour from the air before the temperature is taken down to −200 °C?
  ....
  .... **(2 marks)**
  (ii) Which of the gases will not become liquids at −200 °C?
  .... **(2 marks)**
  (iii) Which two gases are difficult to separate by this method?
  .... **(2 marks)**
  (iv) Explain your answer to part **(iii)**.
  ....
  ....(1 mark)

(d) Explain how the liquid air is separated by fractional distillation.
....
....
....
.... **(4 marks)**

(e) Which two gases are likely to be found in small quantities within the first gas to be produced in the distillation process? ....
.... **(2 marks)**

■ Exam focus

1 Water is very good at dissolving substances. It is, therefore, very unusual to find really pure water on this planet. The questions that follow are about the purification of water from a reservoir.

  (a) (i) How is filtration of the water from the reservoir carried out?

  .... [1]

  (ii) What is the purpose of filtering at this stage?

  .... [1]

  (b) Chlorine is added to the water near the end of the purification process. Why is chlorine added?

  .... [1]

  (c) Chlorine produces an acidic solution containing two acids. The incomplete chemical equation is shown below. The acid shown as a product is called chloric(I) acid.

  $Cl_2(g) + H_2O(l) \rightarrow$ .... $(aq) + HOCl(aq)$

  What are the name and formula of the other acid that is produced?

  .... [2]

  (d) Why is sodium hydroxide added after chlorination?

  .... [1]

  (e) To prevent tooth decay, an ion is often added to the water before it is supplied to homes. Name this ion and give its formula.

  .... [2]

  (f) (i) Tap water usually contains some chloride ions rather than chlorine. Describe a chemical test which would show that tap water does contain chloride ions.

  ....

  .... [3]

  (ii) Explain in terms of electronic configurations what happens to chlorine when it is converted into chloride ions.

  ....

  ....

  ....

  .... [3]

  [Total: 14]

ATMOSPHERE AND OCEANS

93

2 Active volcanoes produce many substances that are thrown out into the atmosphere. The table below shows the percentages of the gases coming from an active volcano in Iceland. The temperature just inside the volcano is above 1000 °C.

Name of gas	Percentage of gas
Nitrogen	3.2
Water	35.6
Sulfur dioxide	11.7
Carbon dioxide	47.4
Hydrogen	0.39
Carbon monoxide	1.71

(a) Scientists now recognise that the early atmosphere of the Earth came from active volcanoes.

(i) Use the table above to decide which gas is present in the largest quantity in the gases that come from the volcano. Write down its name and its formula.

.... [2]

(ii) Which process do you think causes the removal of much of this gas from the atmosphere?

.... [1]

(iii) Give three important differences between the quantities of gases from the Icelandic volcano and those in our modern atmosphere.

....

.... [4]

(b) Explain why water is in the gas phase when it comes out of the volcano.

.... [1]

(c) The Earth's early atmosphere contained a large proportion of water vapour. Explain what you think happened to all this water vapour.

....

.... [3]

(d) The first oceans were quite acidic. Name and give the formulae of two acids which may have been present in these oceans.

....

.... [4]

[Total: 15]

11 Rates of reaction

1 (a) Chemical reactions occur faster at higher temperatures. Explain why this is the case.

   ....

   ....

   ....

   .... (4 marks)

   (b) State four other factors which may affect the rate at which a chemical reaction occurs.

   ....

   ....

   .... (4 marks)

   (c) Explain the meaning of each of the following terms.
   (i) activation energy

   ....

   .... (2 marks)

   (ii) successful collision

   ....

   .... (2 marks)

2 Explain each of the following using the collision theory.
   (a) Reactions in solution occur faster if the solution has a high concentration.

   ....

   ....

   .... (3 marks)

   (b) Powdered zinc metal reacts faster with hydrochloric acid to give hydrogen gas than strips of zinc metal do.

   ....

   ....

   .... (3 marks)

   (c) A catalyst increases the rate of a chemical reaction.

   ....

   ....

   .... (3 marks)

3 The graphs below were produced by carrying out reactions between sulfuric acid and 2g of magnesium in five different experiments.

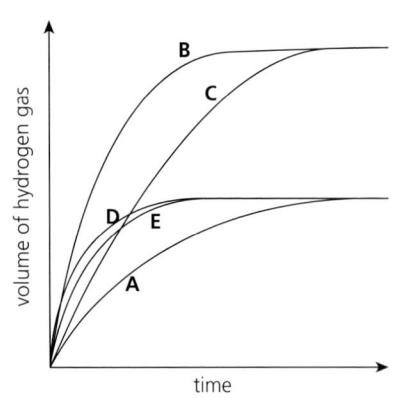

[Graph showing volume of hydrogen gas vs time, with curves labelled A, B, C, D, E]

The experiments carried out involved:

I   2g of magnesium ribbon and 40 cm^3 of 0.1 mol dm^{-3} sulfuric acid at 25 °C
II 2g of magnesium ribbon and 40 cm^3 of 0.05 mol dm^{-3} sulfuric acid at 25 °C
III 2g of magnesium powder and 40 cm^3 of 0.1 mol dm^{-3} sulfuric acid at 25 °C
IV 2g of magnesium powder and 20 cm^3 of 0.1 mol dm^{-3} sulfuric acid at 25 °C
V   2g of magnesium powder and 20 cm^3 of 0.1 mol dm^{-3} sulfuric acid at 50 °C.

(a) Which of the two reactants is in excess?

....

.... (2 marks)

(b) In the table below, write in the number of the experiment which is represented by each of the lines on the graph.

Line	A	B	C	D	E
Experiment					

(5 marks)

(c) Explain why the reaction shown by line **B** occurs more rapidly than the reaction shown by line **C**.

....

....

.... (2 marks)

(d) Explain why the reaction shown by line **D** occurs more rapidly than the reaction shown by line **E**.

....

....

.... (2 marks)

4 Magnesium metal and hydrochloric acid react together to give magnesium chloride and hydrogen gas.

(a) Write a balanced chemical equation for this reaction.

.... (3 marks)

(b) Give a method by which you could follow the rate at which this reaction occurs.

....

.... (2 marks)

(c) Give two ways by which this reaction could be:
  (i) speeded up

....

.... (2 marks)

  (ii) slowed down.

....

.... (2 marks)

5 Hydrogen peroxide can be quickly decomposed to water and oxygen gas by adding the catalyst manganese(IV) oxide or by using the enzyme catalase.

(a) How do both of these substances speed up the decomposition of hydrogen peroxide?

....

.... (2 marks)

(b) Draw an energy level diagram to show what you have described in your answer to part **(a)**.

(3 marks)

(c) Why does catalase not speed up the reaction when the temperature is raised above 40 °C?

....

....

.... (3 marks)

6 A student carried out a reaction between dilute hydrochloric acid and marble chips (calcium carbonate, $CaCO_3$) of different sizes. He placed a conical flask containing 50 cm³ of hydrochloric acid solution onto a digital balance and then added 10 g of large marble chips. He inserted a piece of cotton wool into the neck of the flask. He recorded the loss in mass (in grams) against time.

He repeated the experiment but this time used 10 g of smaller marble chips.

His results are shown in the table below.

Time/min	Loss in mass/g 10 g of large marble chips	Loss in mass/g 10 g of small marble chips
0	0	0
½	0.22	0.45
1	0.41	0.82
1½	0.59	1.15
2	0.78	1.35
2½	0.93	1.50
3	1.07	1.61
3½	1.14	1.66
4	1.23	1.68
4½	1.28	1.69
5	1.35	1.70
5½	1.40	1.70
6	1.44	1.70
6½	1.47	1.70

(a) Write a balanced chemical equation for the reaction between the marble chips and hydrochloric acid.

.... (3 marks)

(b) What was the purpose of the cotton wool which the student placed into the neck of the flask?

....

.... (2 marks)

(c) Why did the mass decrease?

.... (1 mark)

(d) Plot a graph of the loss in mass (vertical axis) against time (horizontal axis). You will need to draw two lines on the same axes, one for the small chips and one for the large chips.

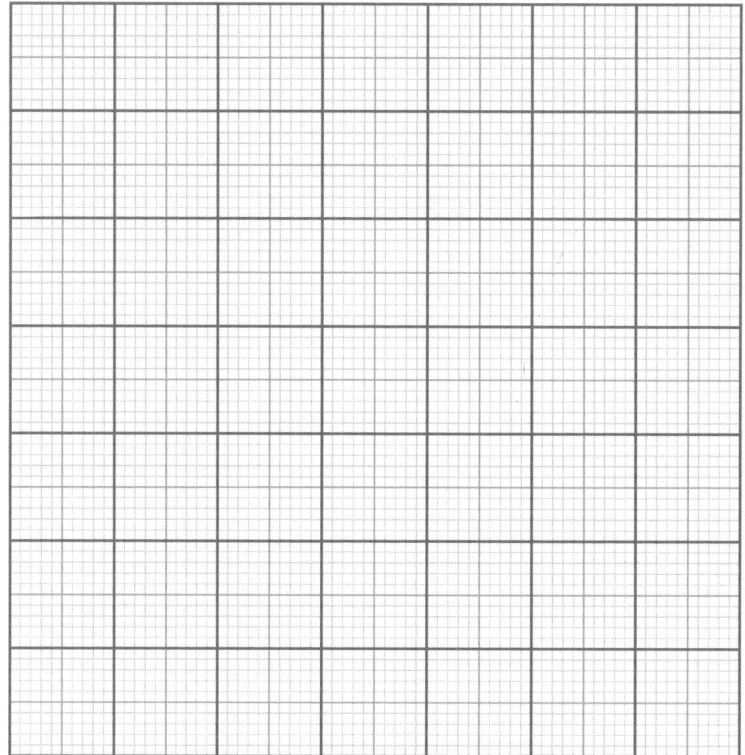

(4 marks)

(e) Which of the reactions was the fastest? How can you tell this from the graph?

....
.... (2 marks)

7 When zinc metal reacts with dilute hydrochloric acid, hydrogen gas is produced. A student recorded the time for 50 cm³ of hydrogen gas to be collected. He carried out the reaction at different temperatures. The results of the various experiments are shown in the table.

Temperature/°C	Time to collect 50 cm³ of hydrogen gas/s	Rate/s^{-1}
20	310	0.32×10^{-2}
30	155	
40	76	1.32×10^{-2}
50	37	
60	19	
70	10	

(a) Write a balanced chemical equation for the reaction of zinc metal with dilute hydrochloric acid.

.... (3 marks)

(b) Complete the table by calculating and writing in the rate for each of the other experiments. (2 marks)

(c) Plot a graph of the rate (vertical axis) against temperature (horizontal axis).

(4 marks)

(d) What is the rate of reaction at:

(i) 45 °C? ....

(ii) 65 °C? .... (2 marks)

(e) Use your graph to find the time it would have taken for 50 cm³ of hydrogen gas to be collected at:

(i) 35 °C ....

(ii) 55 °C. .... (4 marks)

8 A student carried out a reaction between sodium and water. The results she obtained are shown in the table below.

Time/s	0	10	20	30	40	50	60	70	80
Volume of $H_2(g)/cm^3$	0	13	25	36	45	48	50	50	50

(a) Plot a graph of the volume of hydrogen produced (vertical axis) against time (horizontal axis).

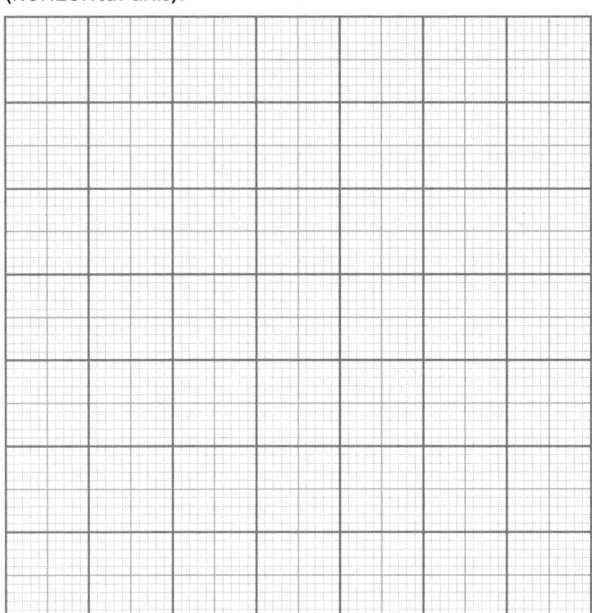

(4 marks)

(b) (i) When was the reaction the fastest?
.... (1 mark)

(ii) How can you tell this from the graph?
.... (1 mark)

(c) Write a balanced chemical equation for the reaction between sodium and water.
.... (3 marks)

(d) What mass of sodium did the student use in the experiment?
....
.... (3 marks)

(e) How much hydrogen was produced in the experiment after:

(i) 25 seconds? .... (1 mark)

(ii) 65 seconds? .... (1 mark)

(f) Which other Group 1 metal could the student have used, instead of sodium, to give a slower reaction with water?
.... (1 mark)

Stretch and challenge

9 Cars are now fitted with catalytic converters to prevent carbon monoxide and nitrogen monoxide gases from passing into the atmosphere with the exhaust gases. The catalyst speeds up the reaction between carbon monoxide and nitrogen monoxide to produce carbon dioxide and nitrogen.

(a) Write a balanced chemical equation for the reaction between carbon monoxide and nitrogen monoxide gas.

.... (3 marks)

(b) The reaction you have written in part (a) shows both oxidation and reduction. Which of the reactants has been:

(i) oxidised? .... (1 mark)

(ii) reduced? .... (1 mark)

(c) What catalyst is used in the catalytic converter?

.... (1 mark)

(d) 5 dm³ of petrol is combusted in a car engine. Assume that it is octane (C_8H_{18}), which has a density of 0.70 g cm⁻³.

(i) Write a balanced chemical equation for the combustion of octane.

.... (3 marks)

(ii) Calculate the mass of carbon dioxide which would be produced.

....
.... (3 marks)

(iii) What would be the total volume of carbon dioxide gas that would be produced?

....
.... (2 marks)

(iv) If the car produced 100 g of carbon monoxide, what mass of carbon dioxide would this be converted to in the catalytic converter?

....
.... (3 marks)

10 A student was trying to find out which of two transition metal oxides would be the best catalyst to decompose hydrogen peroxide (H_2O_2). Hydrogen peroxide is a colourless solution which decomposes to give water and oxygen gas.

(a) What is a catalyst?

.... (2 marks)

(b) Write a balanced chemical equation for the decomposition of hydrogen peroxide.

.... (3 marks)

(c) The table below shows the student's results.

Time/s		0	30	60	90	120	150	180	210	240
Volume of oxygen gas collected/cm³	5 g of manganese(IV) oxide	0	9	17	23	26	28	29	30	30
	5 g of copper(II) oxide	0	3	5	7	9	11	13	15	17

Plot a graph of the volume of oxygen produced (vertical axis) against time (horizontal axis). You will need to draw two lines on the same axes.

Stretch and challenge

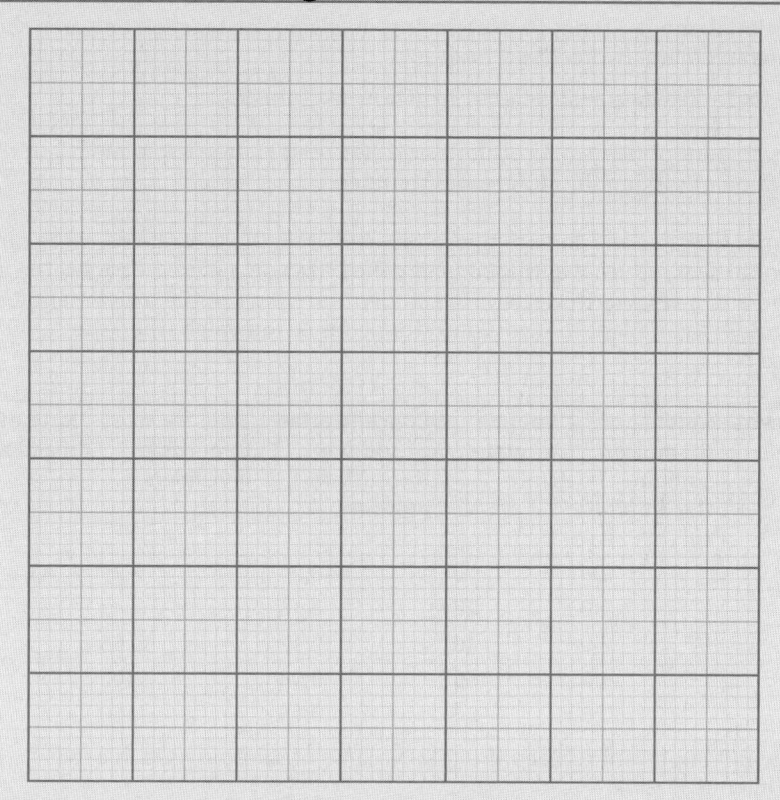

(6 marks)

(d) Which of the two catalysts is the best? Explain your answer.

.... (2 marks)

(e) Draw an apparatus which could be used to carry out this experiment.

(4 marks)

(f) What mass of copper(II) oxide would be obtained at the end of the experiment? Explain your answer.

....

.... (3 marks)

103

Exam focus

1 This question is about a series of experiments involving the reaction between sodium thiosulfate and dilute hydrochloric acid.

$Na_2S_2O_3(aq) + 2HCl(aq) \rightarrow 2NaCl(aq) + H_2O(l) + SO_2(g) + S(s)$

The same amount of dilute hydrochloric acid was used in each experiment but the concentration of sodium thiosulfate was changed.

The volumes of water and sodium thiosulfate shown in the table below were put into a conical flask, which was placed on a pencil cross on a piece of paper. The acid was added and a stopwatch started. The student carrying out the experiment looked down through the flask at the cross and stopped the stopwatch when she could no longer see it.

Experiment	Volume of 0.2 mol dm^{-3} sodium thiosulfate/cm^3	Volume of water/cm^3	Concentration of sodium thiosulfate/mol dm^{-3}	Time for cross to become invisible/s	Rate of reaction/s^{-1}
1	100	0	0.2	25	4.0 × 10^{-2}
2	80	20	0.16	43	
3	60	40	0.12	65	
4	40	60	0.08	102	
5	20	80	0.04	160	

(a) Why was it important to keep the total volume of solution used in each experiment the same?

....

.... [2]

(b) Why did it become more difficult to see the cross on the paper as the reaction proceeded?

....

.... [2]

(c) Complete the table by calculating and writing in the rate of reaction for each of experiments **2** to **5**. [4]

(d) Plot a graph of the rate of reaction (vertical axis) against concentration of sodium thiosulfate (horizontal axis).

[4]

(e) Use your graph to find:
  (i) the concentration of sodium thiosulfate for which the cross would become invisible after 50 seconds
  .... [1]
  (ii) the volume of sodium thiosulfate for which the cross would become invisible after 90 seconds
  .... [1]
  (iii) the time you would expect if the concentration of sodium thiosulfate in the conical flask was 0.10 mol dm^{-3}.
  .... [1]

[Total: 15]

2 Michael carried out a series of reactions between zinc metal and dilute sulfuric acid. In each of the reactions he used the same mass of zinc (an excess) and the same volume of sulfuric acid. The graph below shows his results.

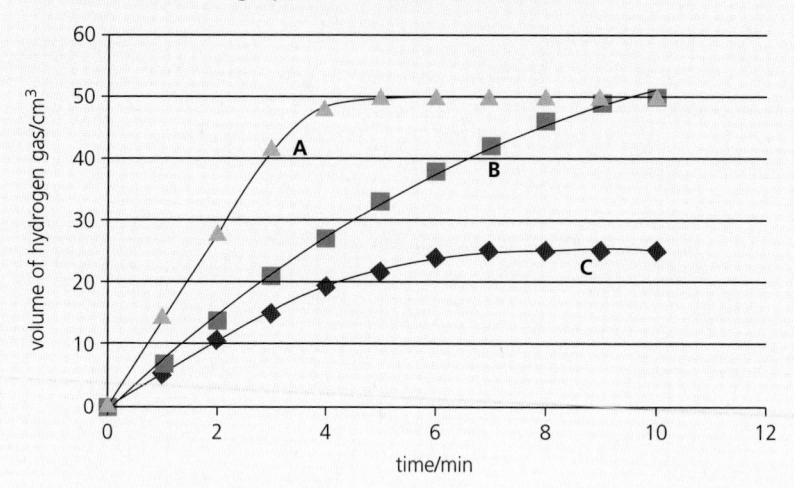

(a) Which was the fastest reaction? Explain how you can tell this from the graph.

....

.... [2]

(b) Which of the reactions was carried out:
  (i) at the highest temperature?

  .... [1]

  (ii) using sulfuric acid of half the concentration used in the other two?

  .... [1]

(c) How could the rate of reaction **A** have been increased?

.... [1]

(d) What volume of 0.05 mol dm^{-3} sulfuric acid was used for reaction **C**?

....

....

.... [3]

(e) What was the total mass of hydrogen gas produced in reaction **A**?

....

....

.... [2]

[Total: 10]

12 The petroleum industry

1 Crude oil is a very important mixture. There are many substances in this mixture which are used as fuels or as the starting materials for the production of a variety of important chemicals. Oil can be separated by fractional distillation. A simplified diagram of this process is shown below.

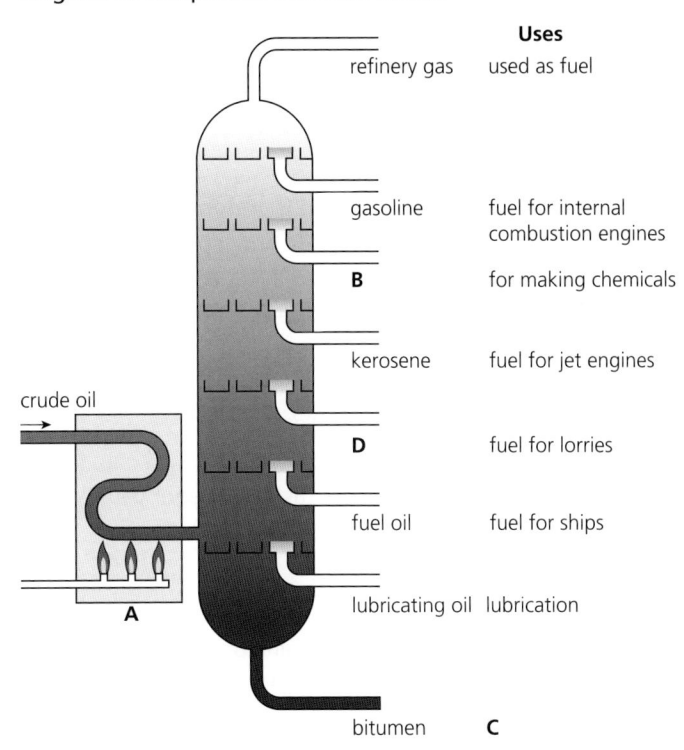

Fraction	Uses
refinery gas	used as fuel
gasoline	fuel for internal combustion engines
B	for making chemicals
kerosene	fuel for jet engines
D	fuel for lorries
fuel oil	fuel for ships
lubricating oil	lubrication
bitumen	C

(a) Why are oil refineries usually found near ports?

.... (1 mark)

(b) (i) What change to the crude oil takes place in part **A**?

.... (2 marks)

   (ii) Name the fraction **B**. .... (1 mark)

   (iii) Give the use **C**. .... (1 mark)

   (iv) Name the fraction **D**. .... (1 mark)

(c) Which of the fractions shown in the diagram contains:

   (i) the biggest molecules? .... (1 mark)

   (ii) the smallest molecules? .... (1 mark)

(d) Which of the fractions represents liquids with the lowest boiling points?

.... (1 mark)

(e) The gasoline is itself a mixture of substances. How are these different substances separated?

.... (1 mark)

2 The table below shows information about several fractions from the distillation of crude oil.

Fraction	Approximate percentage in crude oil	Approximate percentage demand
Refinery gas	2	5
Gasoline	21	28
Kerosene	13	8
Diesel oil	17	25
Fuel oil and bitumen	47	34

(a) Which fractions are in the greatest demand generally?

.... (3 marks)

(b) (i) Which of the fractions has the lowest demand and is present in the smallest amount in crude oil?

.... (1 mark)

(ii) What is the comparative size of the molecules of the compounds in this fraction?

.... (1 mark)

(c) What is the total demand for fuels for cars and lorries?

.... (1 mark)

(d) Using the data from the table, explain how an oil industry manager could ensure that the demand for diesel and gasoline is met.

....

.... (2 marks)

(e) Using the data from the table, what do you think the oil industry manager would do to ensure that the excess of the fuel oil and bitumen fraction is not wasted?

.... (2 marks)

3 (a) Alkanes are unreactive compounds. They are not affected by many substances. Name two common classes of substance that they do not react with.

.... (2 marks)

(b) The most important property of alkanes is that they will generally burn quite easily. The gaseous alkanes are some of the most useful fuels. When a gas like methane burns in a plentiful supply of air, which type of combustion does it undergo?

.... (1 mark)

(c) What is the common name for methane? .... (1 mark)

(d) The balanced chemical equation for the burning of methane in a plentiful supply of air is given below.

$$CH_4(g) + 2O_2(g) \rightarrow CO_2(g) + 2H_2O(g) \qquad \Delta H = -ve$$

(i) What does the sign of ΔH tell you about the reaction?
.... (1 mark)

(ii) How many moles of carbon dioxide are produced by 1 mole of methane?
.... (1 mark)

(iii) What mass of carbon dioxide would be produced by 64 g of methane burning in a plentiful supply of air? (A_r values: H = 1; C = 12; O = 16)
....
.... (2 marks)

(iv) What volume of carbon dioxide would be produced when 100 dm³ of methane is burned in a plentiful supply of air? (1 mole of any gas occupies 24 dm³ at room temperature and pressure.)
....
.... (2 marks)

4 *Cracking* using a *catalyst* is one of the most important chemical processes carried out by the oil industry. Cracking involves the *thermal decomposition* of the fractions containing the larger *alkane* molecules. The process produces a mixture of *saturated* and *unsaturated* molecules.

Explain the meaning of each of the following terms.

(a) cracking ....
.... (2 marks)

(b) catalyst ....
.... (2 marks)

(c) thermal decomposition ....
.... (2 marks)

(d) alkane ....
.... (2 marks)

(e) saturated ....
.... (2 marks)

(f) unsaturated ....
.... (2 marks)

5 (a) Name the homologous series represented by the general formula C_nH_{2n}.
.... (1 mark)

(b) Complete the following chemical formulae, which represent molecules that belong to the homologous series in part (a).

$C\_\_H_6$ \qquad $C_8H\_\_$ \qquad $\_\_\_\_\_6\_\_\_\_\_$ \qquad (3 marks)

(c) Draw the structural formula of the first of the molecules shown in part (b).

(2 marks)

6 (a) What structural feature does an alkene possess that an alkane does not?

.... (1 mark)

(b) The diagram below shows the outer energy levels of the elements present in the compound ethene. Complete the bonding diagram by drawing dots and crosses to show the electrons in the overlap areas.

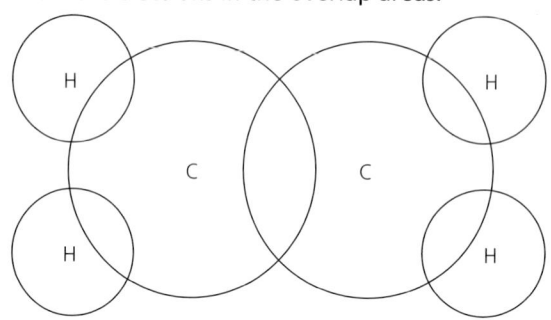

(5 marks)

7 For each of the following statements about methane and ethene, write either 'true' or 'false'.

(a) Methane is a greenhouse gas. .... (1 mark)

(b) Methane is added to the atmosphere by burning fossil fuels. .... (1 mark)

(c) Ethene is used for making a commonly used plastic. .... (1 mark)

(d) Methane cannot be cracked. .... (1 mark)

(e) Ethene contains a triple covalent bond. .... (1 mark)

(f) Ethene does not burn easily. .... (1 mark)

8 Draw lines to link each molecule on the left with the correct statement on the right.

(a) $C_2H_2Br_2$	A Contains a total of 12 atoms
(b) C_2H_5OH	B Undergoes addition reactions
(c) O_3	C Formed in cracking
(d) C_3H_7OH	D Undergoes substitution reactions
(e) C_5H_{10}	E Produced in a test for an alkene
(f) C_2H_6	F Reacts with chlorine atoms in the upper atmosphere
(g) H_2	G Produced when ethene reacts with steam

(7 marks)

Stretch and challenge

9 Give the name and structural formula of the main organic product(s) formed when each of the following chemical procedures is carried out.

(a) A mixture of equal amounts of methane and chlorine is exposed to ultraviolet light.

.... (2 marks)

(b) A mixture of ethene and steam is passed over an acid catalyst at high temperature and pressure.

.... (2 marks)

(c) A mixture of ethene and hydrogen is passed over a metal catalyst at a high temperature.

.... (2 marks)

(d) Ethene is bubbled into a solution of bromine in 1,1,1-trichloroethane.

.... (2 marks)

(e) Decane is passed over a heated catalyst.

.... (4 marks)

10 (a) Explain the meaning of the term *isomer* with reference to the molecule C_4H_{10}. Name and draw the structures of any substances you include in your answer.

....
....
....
.... (6 marks)

Stretch and challenge

(b) (i) What would you expect to be the relative boiling points of the isomers you have drawn in part **(a)**?

.... (1 mark)

(ii) Explain why the isomers you have drawn in part **(a)** have different boiling points.

....

.... (2 marks)

(c) Explain why there is an extremely large number of organic compounds.

.... (1 mark)

(d) Carvone is an organic substance which is found in fresh mint and in caraway seeds. The taste is created by the presence of carvone in both, but they have different tastes. Explain why the taste is so different.

....

.... (2 marks)

■ Exam focus

1 (a) The alkanes form a homologous series of hydrocarbons obtained from crude oil. What do you understand by the terms *homologous series* and *hydrocarbons*?

....

....

....

.... [5]

(b) (i) The first four members of the alkane family are shown in the table below.

Alkane	Formula	Structure
Methane		H–C–H (with H above and below)
Ethane	C_2H_6	
Propane		H–C–C–C–H (with H's above and below each C)
Butane		

Complete the table by filling in the missing formulae and structures. [5]

(ii) Name the type of bonding present in alkanes. .... [2]

(iii) By showing the outer electron energy levels, draw a diagram to show the chemical bonding in a molecule of ethane.

[4]

(iv) All the alkanes shown in the table above are gases. What would be the physical difference between these four alkanes and the alkane decane, $C_{10}H_{22}$?
.... [1]

(v) What is the general formula for the alkane series? .... [1]

[Total: 18]

2 The diagram shows the apparatus used in the cracking of a liquid alkane. Some of the labels have been replaced with numbers.

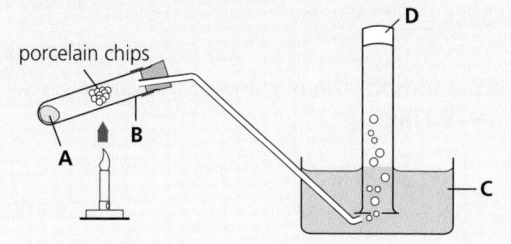

(a) For each letter, write down the correct label from the list below.

> gaseous alkene   hard glass boiling tube
> paraffin-soaked mineral wool   water

A ....

B ....

C ....

D .... [4]

(b) What is the purpose of the porcelain chips in this experiment?
.... [2]

(c) Give an explanation of the following observation: 'The substance collected in the test-tube was found to decolorise bromine dissolved in an organic solvent.'
....
....
.... [3]

(d) Draw a star on the diagram above to show the position where you would introduce a further piece of apparatus to collect any liquid product. [1]

(e) An explosive element gas can also be produced in this process. Give the name and formula of this gas.
.... [2]

(f) (i) Complete the following symbol equation for a possible cracking of dodecane.

$C_{12}H_{26} \rightarrow C_4H_8 +$ .... [1]

(ii) Name the products of the reaction shown in the equation in part (i).
.... [2]

[Total: 15]

13 Energy sources

1. **(a)** What is a *fuel*?

   .... (2 marks)

   (b) Give four properties of a good fuel.

   ....

   .... (4 marks)

   (c) Name:

   (i) a liquid fuel .... (1 mark)

   (ii) a solid fuel .... (1 mark)

   (iii) a gaseous fuel. .... (1 mark)

   (d) Write word and balanced chemical equations for the burning of the gaseous fuel you have named in your answer to part **(c) (iii)**.

   ....

   .... (4 marks)

2. Complete the table below by writing in two advantages and two disadvantages of each of the following alternative sources of energy.

Source	Advantages	Disadvantages
Nuclear power	1 2	1 2
Wave power	1 2	1 2
Hydroelectric power	1 2	1 2
Wind power	1 2	1 2

(16 marks)

3 The reaction between methane and oxygen is exothermic. The standard heat of combustion of methane is −728 kJ mol⁻¹.

$$CH_4(g) + 2O_2(g) \rightarrow CO_2(g) + 2H_2O(l) \quad \Delta H = -728 \text{ kJ mol}^{-1}$$

(a) Calculate the amount of energy produced when each of the following amounts of methane is completely combusted.

   (i) 2 moles of methane .... (1 mark)

   (ii) 0.25 mole of methane .... (1 mark)

   (iii) 8 g of methane .... (1 mark)

   (iv) 64 g of methane .... (1 mark)

(b) Draw an energy level diagram to represent the complete combustion of 1 mole of methane.

(3 marks)

4 Use the bond energy data given in the table below to answer this question.

Bond	Bond energy/kJ mol^{-1}
C—H	413
O=O	498
C=O	805
H—O	464
C—C	347

(a) Calculate the enthalpy of combustion of propane.
$C_3H_8(g) + 5O_2(g) \rightarrow 3CO_2(g) + 4H_2O(g)$

....

....

....

....

....

.... (6 marks)

(b) Draw an energy level diagram to represent this combustion process.

(3 marks)

(c) How much energy is released when each of the following amounts of propane is burned? (A_r values: H = 1; C = 12)

(i) 0.5 mole of propane

.... (1 mark)

(ii) 5 moles of propane

.... (1 mark)

(iii) 11 g of propane

.... (1 mark)

5 Water is formed and energy is released when hydrogen combines with oxygen.

   (a) Write a balanced chemical equation, including state symbols, for this reaction.

   .... **(4 marks)**

   (b) In this reaction, the covalent bonds in the molecules of hydrogen and oxygen are broken. Is the bond breaking process exothermic or endothermic? Explain your answer.

   ....

   .... **(2 marks)**

   (c) Use the bond energies in the table below to calculate the energy change for the reaction you have shown in part **(a)**.

Bond	Bond energy/kJ mol^{-1}
H—H	436
O=O	498
O—H	464

   .... **(5 marks)**

6 The table below gives the enthalpies of combustion of four alcohols.

Alcohol	Molecular formula	Enthalpy of combustion/kJ mol^{-1}
Methanol	CH$_3$OH	−726
Ethanol	C$_2$H$_5$OH	−1370
Propan-1-ol	C$_3$H$_7$OH	−2010
Butan-1-ol	C$_4$H$_9$OH	−2670

(a) Plot a graph of the enthalpy of combustion against relative molecular mass for these four alcohols.

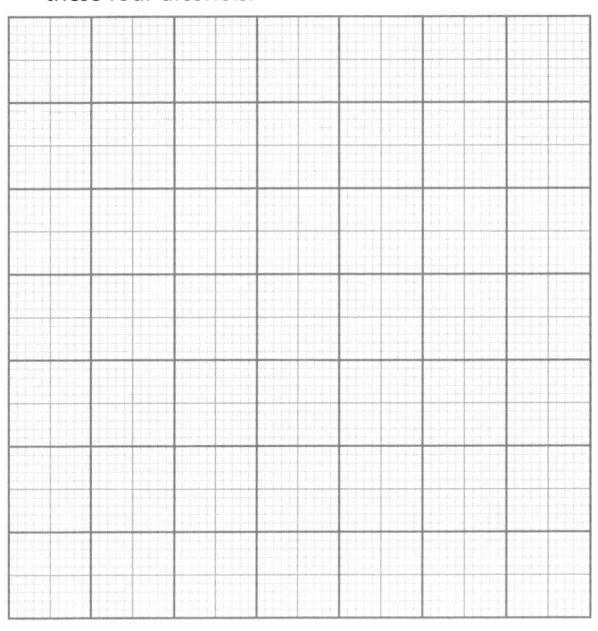

(4 marks)

(b) (i) From your graph, predict the enthalpy change of combustion of pentan-1-ol. .... (2 marks)

(ii) Explain how you obtained your answer to part (i).

....

.... (2 marks)

(c) What can you say about the energy produced when alcohols of progressively higher molecular mass are burned in air?

.... (1 mark)

7 In some countries, including Brazil, ethanol is mixed with petrol.

(a) (i) Write a balanced chemical equation for the complete combustion of ethanol.

.... (3 marks)

(ii) Use the bond energy data in the table on the next page to calculate the enthalpy of combustion of ethanol.

Bond	Bond energy/kJ mol⁻¹
C—H	413
O=O	498
C=O	805
H—O	464
C—C	347
C—O	358

(5 marks)

(b) In the manufacture of cars, an important factor which is considered is known as the *energy density*. This is the amount of energy released when 1 kg of the fuel is burned, and it can be used to compare the energy efficiencies of different fuels. Using your answer to part **(a) (ii)** and given that the enthalpy of combustion of hydrogen gas is −286 kJ mol⁻¹, calculate the energy density of both hydrogen and ethanol in kJ kg⁻¹.

(4 marks)

(c) Compare the energy density of hydrogen with that of ethanol and give a reason for the difference.

....

.... (3 marks)

8 The enthalpy of neutralisation is the enthalpy change which takes place when 1 mole of hydrogen ions (H⁺(aq)) are neutralised.

H⁺(aq) + OH⁻(aq) → H₂O(l)   ΔH = −57 kJ mol⁻¹

This process occurs, for example, in the titration of an alkali by an acid to produce a neutral solution.

How much energy is released when:

(a) 2 moles of hydrogen ions are neutralised?

.... (1 mark)

(b) 0.25 mole of hydrogen ions are neutralised?

.... (1 mark)

(c) 1 mole of sulfuric acid is completely neutralised?

....

.... (3 marks)

(d) 2 moles of sodium hydroxide are neutralised?

.... (1 mark)

Stretch and challenge

9 Use the bond energies in the table below to help you answer this question.

Bond	Bond energy/kJ mol^{-1}
C—H	413
O=O	498
C=O	805
H—O	464
C—C	347
C=C	612
C—O	358
H—H	454

(a) (i) Write a balanced chemical equation for the reaction of ethene with hydrogen to form ethane.

.... (2 marks)

(ii) Calculate the energy change for the reaction between ethene and hydrogen.

(5 marks)

(b) (i) Write a balanced chemical equation for the reaction of ethene with water to form ethanol.

.... (2 marks)

(ii) Calculate the energy change for the reaction between ethene and water.

(5 marks)

Stretch and challenge

10 The diagram below shows an electrochemical cell which is based on the *first ever* chemical cell.

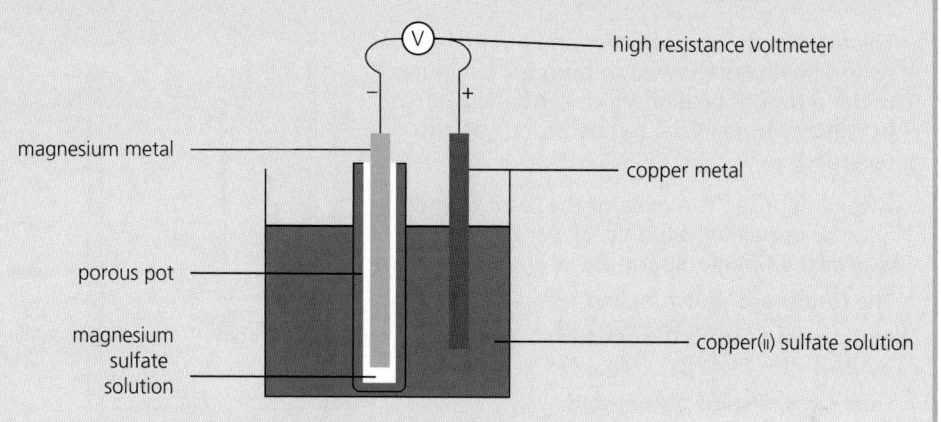

(a) The electrode reaction taking place at the anode is:
$Cu^{2+}(aq) + 2e^- \rightarrow Cu(s)$
Does this equation show oxidation or reduction? Explain your answer.
.... **(2 marks)**

(b) Write an equation to show what occurs at the cathode, including state symbols.
.... **(4 marks)**

(c) Which way would the electrons flow in the wire – from copper to magnesium or from magnesium to copper?
....**(1 mark)**

(d) What carries the electric current through the solutions?
....**(1 mark)**

(e) What is the purpose of the porous pot?
....**(1 mark)**

Exam focus

1 An experiment was carried out to determine the enthalpy of combustion of butan-1-ol. The apparatus that was used is shown below. The heat source was a spirit burner containing butan-1-ol.

The mass of the spirit burner and butan-1-ol was recorded. It was allowed to burn for 4 minutes under a copper beaker which contained 500 cm³ of water, whose initial temperature was also recorded.

After 4 minutes, the mass of the spirit burner and the remaining butan-1-ol was recorded *as well as* the final temperature of the water.

The results are shown below.

Initial mass of spirit burner and butan-1-ol = 29.42 g

Final mass of spirit burner and butan-1-ol = 27.51 g

Initial temperature of the water = 21.2 °C

Final temperature of the water = 42.0 °C

(a) What mass of butan-1-ol was burned during the experiment?

.... [1]

(b) What was the temperature rise of the water during the experiment?

.... [1]

(c) Use the following relationship to find the energy transferred during the experiment in joules. (The density of water is 1 g cm⁻³.)

energy transferred = mass of water × 4.2 × temperature rise

[3]

(d) How many moles of butan-1-ol were burned during the experiment? (A_r values: H = 1; C = 12; O = 16)

....

.... [3]

(e) Using the results from this experiment, what is the enthalpy of combustion of butan-1-ol?

....

.... [3]

[Total: 11]

2 Hydrazine, H₂N—NH₂, has been used as a rocket fuel for many years. When it burns in oxygen gas, it reacts to form nitrogen gas and water as the only products.

(a) Write a balanced chemical equation for the combustion of hydrazine.

.... [3]

(b) When hydrazine undergoes combustion, a lot of energy is produced. Use the bond energies in the table below to calculate the magnitude of this energy change.

Bond	Bond energy/kJ mol⁻¹
N—H	390
N—N	158
N≡N	946
O—H	464
O=O	498

[5]

(c) If 240 kg of hydrazine was burned completely, what amount of heat energy would be released? (A_r values: H = 1; N = 14)

[3]

[Total: 11]

14 The (wider) organic manufacturing industry

1. When small molecules such as ethene join together to form long chains of atoms, called *polymers,* the process is called *polymerisation*. The small molecules like ethene, which join together in this way, are called *monomers*. The polymer formed with ethene is an *addition polymer.* Polymers are often referred to as *macromolecules*. Explain the meaning of each of the following terms.

   (a) polymer ....

   ....

   ....

   .... (2 marks)

   (b) polymerisation ....

   ....

   ....

   ....

   .... (2 marks)

   (c) monomer ....

   ....

   ....

   .... (2 marks)

   (d) addition polymer ....

   ....

   ....

   .... (2 marks)

   (e) macromolecule ....

   ....

   ....

   .... (1 mark)

2. (a) Other addition polymers include PVC and PTFE. Give the chemical name of:

   (i) PVC .... (1 mark)

   (ii) PTFE. .... (1 mark)

(b) Name and draw the monomer unit that each of these polymers is made from.
   (i) PVC

   (2 marks)

   (ii) PTFE

   (2 marks)

(c) Draw part of the polymer chain for each of these two addition polymers.
   (i) PVC

   (1 mark)

   (ii) PTFE

   (1 mark)

(d) Give two uses for:
   (i) PVC
   .... (2 marks)
   (ii) PTFE.
   .... (2 marks)

3 For each of the following statements about addition polymers, write either 'true' or 'false'.

(a) They are generally thermosoftening. .... (1 mark)

(b) They cannot be recycled. .... (1 mark)

(c) The price of these polymers is dependent on the price of oil. .... (1 mark)

(d) Especially high temperatures need to be used for their safe incineration.

.... (1 mark)

(e) Ethene is the starting material for many addition polymers. .... (1 mark)

(f) The chains in addition polymers can easily pass over each other when the plastic is stretched. .... (1 mark)

4 (a) Name the polymerisation process that is used to make both nylon and Terylene.

.... (1 mark)

(b) Name the starting materials for making:
   (i) nylon

   .... (2 marks)

   (ii) Terylene.

   .... (2 marks)

(c) Give the name and formula of the small molecule produced during the polymerisation reactions to produce both nylon and Terylene.

.... (2 marks)

(d) Give the name of the chemical link that holds together:
   (i) nylon .... (1 mark)

   (ii) Terylene. .... (1 mark)

(e) Give two uses for:
   (i) nylon

   .... (2 marks)

   (ii) Terylene.

   .... (2 marks)

(f) Explain the difference between the type of polymerisation you have named in part **(a)** and addition polymerisation.

....

.... (2 marks)

5 The table below shows some of the properties of the first four alcohols.
   (a) Complete the table by writing in the missing names and formulae.

Alcohol	Formula	Melting point/°C	Boiling point/°C
Methanol		−94	64
	C_2H_5OH	−117	78
Propanol		−126	97
	C_4H_9OH	−89	117

(4 marks)

(b) The functional group of alcohols is –OH. Explain what is meant by the term *functional group*.

.... (2 marks)

(c) By considering the structures of the alcohol molecules, explain why there is an increase in boiling point from methanol to butanol.

....

....

.... (3 marks)

(d) What is the general formula for the homologous series of alcohols?

.... (1 mark)

6 The structure of the cholesterol molecule is shown below.

(a) What type of bonding is present in this molecule? .... (1 mark)
(b) Which part of the molecule will react with:
   (i) steam? .... (1 mark)
   (ii) ethanoic acid? .... (1 mark)
(c) If an addition polymer was to be made with this cholesterol, which part of the molecule would be likely to react?

.... (1 mark)

(d) If a condensation polymer like Terylene was to be made with this cholesterol, which part of the molecule would be likely to react?

.... (1 mark)

7 (a) Starch can undergo a process called hydrolysis. Explain what you understand by the term *hydrolysis*.

....

.... (2 marks)

(b) (i) Identify and give the formulae of the substances **A** to **C** in the chart below, which represents the breaking down of starch and subsequent reactions of the products.

```
                dilute acid          yeast
       Starch  ──────────→  A  ──────────→  B + Carbon dioxide



                acidified
                potassium
                dichromate(VI)
           B   ──────────────→  C + Water
```

A ....

B ....

C ....

(6 marks)

(ii) What test could be used to identify substance **C**?

....

.... (3 marks)

(iii) What type of reagent is potassium dichromate(VI)?

.... (1 mark)

(iv) A different substance will be produced instead of **A** if an enzyme is used in the first stage. Name the different substance that would be produced if an enzyme was used.

.... (1 mark)

(v) Name an enzyme that could be used instead of the dilute acid.

.... (1 mark)

8 Draw lines to link each substance on the left with the correct description on the right.

| (a) C_2H_3Cl |
| (b) C_2H_5OH |
| (c) CH_3COOH |
| (d) $CH_3COOC_2H_5$ |
| (e) Starch |
| (f) $C_6H_{12}O_6$ |
| (g) HCOOH |

| A A monosaccharide |
| B Found in stinging nettles |
| C An ester |
| D Monomer for PVC |
| E A biopolymer |
| F A carboxylic acid |
| G An excellent solvent |

(7 marks)

Stretch and challenge

9 The amount of ethanoic acid in vinegar can be determined by carrying out a titration. The results below came from a titration of a vinegar solution with sodium hydroxide solution. The neutralisation reaction taking place is:

$CH_3COOH(aq) + NaOH(aq) \rightarrow CH_3COONa(aq) + H_2O(l)$

25.00 cm³ of vinegar was just neutralised by 20.00 cm³ of a 0.10 mol dm⁻³ sodium hydroxide solution. Calculate:

(a) the concentration of ethanoic acid in the vinegar solution

(3 marks)

(b) the mass of ethanoic acid in a 1 litre (1 dm³) bottle of this vinegar. (A_r values: H = 1; C = 12; O = 16)

(2 marks)

Stretch and challenge

10 (a) Amino acids are essential for the formation of proteins. How many amino acids are there?

.... (1 mark)

(b) Each amino acid contains two functional groups. What are the names of these functional groups?

.... (2 marks)

(c) The structure of the first amino acid, glycine, is shown below.

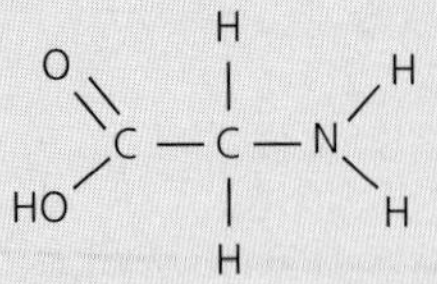

$$\underset{HO}{O=}C-\underset{H}{\overset{H}{C}}-N\underset{H}{\overset{H}{\diagdown}}$$

Redraw the structure to show a bonding diagram for this substance, showing the outer electron energy levels only.

(8 marks)

(d) Amino acids are the building blocks for proteins. Proteins are long-chain molecules or natural polymers.

  (i) Name the polymerisation process that is required to form proteins.

.... (1 mark)

  (ii) Which industrial polymer contains the same link as that found in proteins?

.... (1 mark)

  (iii) The diagram below shows a dipeptide.

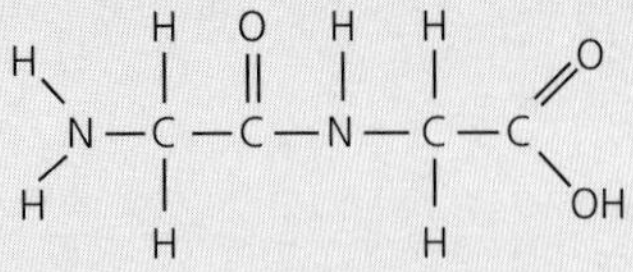

$$H\diagdown \underset{H}{N}-\underset{H}{\overset{H}{C}}-\underset{}{\overset{O}{\overset{\|}{C}}}-\underset{H}{\overset{H}{N}}-\underset{H}{\overset{H}{C}}-C\diagup\overset{O}{\underset{OH}{}}$$

What do you understand by the term *dipeptide*?

.... (1 mark)

  (iv) Draw a circle around the link that holds this dipeptide together.

(1 mark)

Exam focus

1 (a) Ethene, C_2H_4, is the starting material for making plastic carrier bags.

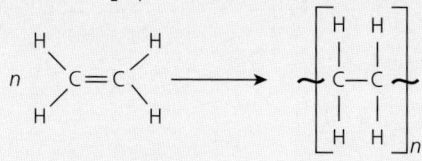

$$n \begin{array}{c} H \\ \diagdown \\ / \\ H \end{array} C=C \begin{array}{c} H \\ \diagup \\ \diagdown \\ H \end{array} \longrightarrow \begin{bmatrix} H & H \\ | & | \\ C-C \\ | & | \\ H & H \end{bmatrix}_n$$

  (i) Name the type of chemical change taking place in the diagram above.

  .... [1]

  (ii) Name the product formed by this reaction.

  .... [1]

  (iii) The alkene, ethene, is made by cracking large alkane molecules. Describe a simple chemical test to show that ethene is present.

  ....
  .... [2]

(b) The majority of carrier bags are difficult to dispose of.
  (i) Explain why carrier bags should not just be thrown away.

  ....
  ....
  .... [4]

  (ii) Explain why the majority of plastic carrier bags are recycled.

  ....
  .... [2]

  (iii) Give one advantage that a plastic carrier bag has over one made out of paper.

  .... [1]

(c) A label like the one below is found on some plastic carrier bags.

> This plastic carrier bag is made from a substance that is made from the chemical elements carbon and hydrogen only. When the carrier bag is burned it produces carbon dioxide and water. These substances are natural and will not harm the environment.

  (i) What is the meaning of the term *element*?

  .... [2]

  (ii) What is the name given to the type of compound that contains the elements carbon and hydrogen only?

  .... [1]

  (iii) When the plastic bag burns, heat energy is given out. What name is used to describe reactions that give out heat energy?

  .... [1]

  (iv) The plastic bag will probably give off a toxic gas when it is burned. Why is this the case?

  ....
  .... [3]

[Total: 18]

2 Ethanol (alcohol) is a product of many fermentation reactions and of the hydration of ethene. The molecular formula of ethanol is C_2H_5OH.

(a) Draw the structural formula of ethanol.

[1]

(b) (i) Balance the following chemical equation for the fermentation reaction.

$C_6H_{12}O_6(aq) \rightarrow$ .... $C_2H_5OH(l)$ + ... $CO_2(g)$ [2]

(ii) Name the substance $C_6H_{12}O_6$.

.... [1]

(iii) Calculate the M_r value for $C_6H_{12}O_6$. (A_r values: C = 12; H = 1; O = 16)

.... [1]

(c) When ethanol is heated with potassium dichromate(VI), it is converted to ethanoic acid.

$C_2H_5OH(l) \rightarrow CH_3COOH(l)$

(i) What type of reaction is this?

.... [1]

(ii) Ethanoic acid belongs to a homologous series of organic acids. What is the name given to this homologous series of acids?

.... [1]

(iii) When ethanoic acid is reacted with ethanol in the presence of a catalyst, a new substance is produced. Give the name and formula of this new substance.

.... [2]

(iv) Name the catalyst you would use for the reaction in part (iii).

.... [1]

(v) The reaction in part (iii) is known as a reversible reaction. Explain the meaning of the term *reversible reaction*.

....

....

....

.... [4]

[Total: 14]

15 Nitrogen

1 Ammonia, NH_3, is manufactured from nitrogen and hydrogen gases in the Haber process.

(a) Draw a dot-and-cross diagram to show the bonding in a molecule of ammonia.

(2 marks)

(b) Write a balanced chemical equation for the production of ammonia by the Haber process.

.... (4 marks)

(c) Look at the energy level diagram below for the Haber process.

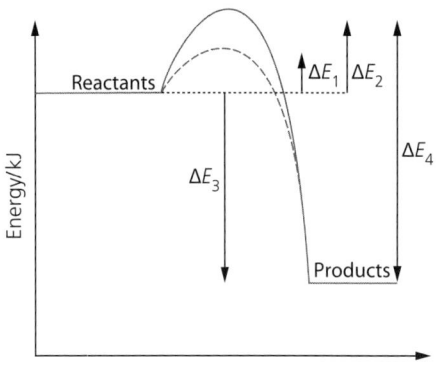

Is the Haber process an exothermic or an endothermic reaction? Using the diagram, explain your answer.

....

.... (3 marks)

(d) Which of the energy changes ΔE_1 to ΔE_4 in the diagram above represents:

  (i) the activation energy for the reaction with a catalyst? .... (1 mark)

  (ii) the energy change (ΔH) for the reaction? .... (1 mark)

  (iii) the activation energy for the reaction without a catalyst?

.... (1 mark)

(e) The Haber process uses a finely divided iron catalyst.
  (i) Why is a catalyst used in the process?
  .... (2 marks)
  (ii) Why is a *finely divided* iron catalyst used?
  .... (2 marks)

2 Nitric acid can be used to make nitrate salts.
  (a) Write balanced chemical equations for the reactions between each of the following pairs of substances.
  (i) nitric acid and potassium hydroxide
  .... (2 marks)
  (ii) nitric acid and sodium carbonate solid
  .... (3 marks)
  (iii) nitric acid and copper(II) oxide
  .... (3 marks)

  (b) Describe how you would carry out a reaction between nitric acid and copper(II) carbonate to make copper(II) nitrate crystals.
  ....
  ....
  ....
  ....
  ....
  .... (6 marks)

3 Look at the reaction scheme below.

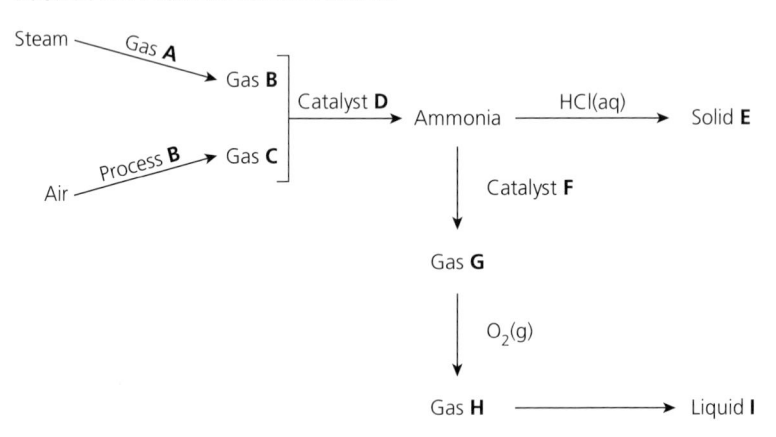

Steam → Gas A → Gas B
Air → Process B → Gas C
Gas B + Gas C → Catalyst D → Ammonia → HCl(aq) → Solid E
Ammonia → Catalyst F → Gas G → O$_2$(g) → Gas H → Liquid I

(a) Give the name and formula of each of the following substances.

   (i) gas **A** ....

   (ii) gas **C** ....

   (iii) gas **G** ....

   (iv) gas **H** .... (8 marks)

(b) Name:

   (i) catalyst **D** ....

   (ii) catalyst **F**. .... (2 marks)

(c) Name and explain process **B** by which gas **C** is obtained from air.

   ....

   .... (3 marks)

(d) Write a balanced chemical equation for the reaction of ammonia and dilute hydrochloric acid.

   .... (2 marks)

(e) Liquid **I** undergoes a neutralisation reaction with sodium hydroxide. Write a balanced chemical equation for the reaction.

   .... (2 marks)

4 Ammonium nitrate fertiliser can be manufactured by reacting aqueous nitric acid with ammonia.

   (a) Write a balanced chemical equation for the reaction.

   .... (2 marks)

   (b) (i) If the process started with 1 tonne of nitric acid, what mass of ammonia would be needed to react with it?

   (3 marks)

(ii) What mass of ammonium nitrate would be made from this reaction?

(3 marks)

(c) What is the percentage of nitrogen in ammonium nitrate?

(2 marks)

5 Ammonia gas can be made in the laboratory by the reaction of an ammonium compound with an alkali using the apparatus shown below.

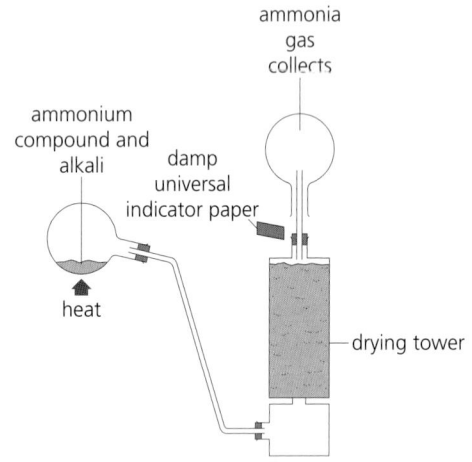

(a) Name a suitable ammonium compound which could be used.

.... (1 mark)

(b) Name a suitable alkali.

.... (1 mark)

(c) Write a balanced chemical equation for the reaction, using the ammonium compound and alkali you have named in your answers to parts **(a)** and **(b)**.

.... (3 marks)

(d) As the ammonia is produced, it is passed through a drying tower to remove water, another product from the reaction. Give the name of a suitable drying agent which could be packed into the tower.

.... (1 mark)

(e) The damp universal indicator paper is used to indicate when the collection vessel is full. What colour would it turn?

.... (1 mark)

(f) By looking at the apparatus, what can you say about the density of ammonia gas?

.... (1 mark)

6 A titration was carried out using 0.05 mol dm^{-3} nitric acid solution to find the concentration of a solution of potassium hydroxide.

(a) Describe the steps you would take to carry out the titration.

....

....

....

....

.... (5 marks)

In such a titration, 21.65 cm^3 of the 0.05 mol dm^{-3} nitric acid was needed to neutralise 25.00 cm^3 of potassium hydroxide solution.

(b) Write a balanced chemical equation for the reaction.

.... (2 marks)

(c) How many moles of nitric acid were used in the reaction?

(2 marks)

(d) How many moles of potassium hydroxide would this number of moles of nitric acid react with?

.... (1 mark)

(e) Calculate the concentration of the potassium hydroxide solution.

(2 marks)

NITROGEN

7 Car exhaust fumes contain nitrogen monoxide gas. When ammonia gas is injected into the hot exhaust gases, a reaction occurs which changes nitrogen monoxide, NO, to nitrogen gas as shown in the equation below.

.... NO + ... NH$_3$ → .... N$_2$ + ... H$_2$O

(a) Balance the equation above. (4 marks)

(b) (i) What mass of ammonia would react with 16 g of nitrogen monoxide, NO?

(3 marks)

(ii) What mass of nitrogen gas would be produced?

(2 marks)

(iii) What volume of nitrogen gas would be produced? (1 mole of gas occupies 24 dm^3 at room temperature and pressure.)

(2 marks)

(c) A family car gives out 20 g of nitrogen monoxide per kilometre. What mass of ammonia would be needed to change the nitrogen monoxide produced during a 200 km journey to nitrogen gas?

(2 marks)

8 (a) Nitrogen is one of the three essential elements needed by plants.

   (i) What type of compound in plants, essential for their growth, contains nitrogen? .... (1 mark)

   (ii) What are the other two essential elements needed by plants for healthy growth?
   .... (2 marks)

(b) The nitrogen needed by plants can be obtained by two different routes. Some plants are able to take nitrogen directly from the air whilst others obtain their nitrogen from the soil.

   (i) Name a plant which is able to take nitrogen directly from the air.
   .... (1 mark)

   (ii) How do farmers ensure that there is sufficient nitrogen in the soil for their crops to grow healthily?
   .... (1 mark)

(c) Calculate the percentage of nitrogen in each of these nitrogen compounds used by farmers.

   (i) sodium nitrate, $NaNO_3$

   (ii) ammonium phosphate, $(NH_4)_3PO_4$

   (iii) urea, $CO(NH_2)_2$

   (iv) ammonium sulfate, $(NH_4)_2SO_4$

(4 marks)

Stretch and challenge

9 Ammonia is a very important industrial chemical. It is used to manufacture fertilisers, dyes and explosives. It is made from nitrogen and hydrogen gases by the Haber process.

(a) Write a balanced chemical equation for the reaction of nitrogen and hydrogen to give ammonia.

.... (4 marks)

(b) In order to produce sufficient ammonia at a fast enough rate from the reaction, certain conditions of temperature and pressure are used. The forward reaction is exothermic.

  (i) At what pressures would the most ammonia be produced? Explain your answer.

  ....
  .... (4 marks)

  (ii) What pressure is used in industry? .... (1 mark)

(c) (i) At what temperatures would the most ammonia be produced? Explain your answer.

  ....
  .... (4 marks)

  (ii) What temperature is used in industry? .... (1 mark)

  (iii) Comment on the difference between your answers to parts (i) and (ii).

  ....
  ....
  .... (3 marks)

(d) What catalyst, other than iron, can be used in the industrial preparation of ammonia?

.... (1 mark)

Stretch and challenge

10 An analytical chemist was asked to identify three colourless solutions which had been found. He carried out various tests in an attempt to identify the solutions. The results of his tests are shown in the table below.

Solution	Flame test colour	Dilute HCl(aq)	Addition of NH_3(aq) Few drops	Addition of NH_3(aq) Excess	Dilute HNO_3(aq) + $AgNO_3$(aq)	Dilute HCl(aq) + $BaCl_2$(aq)
A	Brick red	No reaction	White precipitate	Precipitate dissolves	White precipitate	No reaction
B	Lilac	No reaction	No reaction	No reaction	No reaction	White precipitate
C	Green	Fizzes	Blue precipitate	Precipitate dissolves	Fizzes	Fizzes

(a) Look at the results that were obtained from solution **A**.

  (i) Which metal ion is present in the solution? .... (1 mark)

  (ii) What does the formation of a white precipitate when acidified silver nitrate is added tell you?

  .... (1 mark)

  (iii) Write a balanced ionic equation for the formation of the white precipitate, including state symbols.

  .... (2 marks)

(b) Look at the results that were obtained from solution **B**.

  (i) Which metal ion is present in the solution? .... (1 mark)

  (ii) Which anion must be present for a white precipitate to form when dilute hydrochloric acid and barium chloride solution are added to solution **B**?

  .... (1 mark)

  (iii) Write a balanced ionic equation for the formation of the white precipitate, including state symbols.

  .... (2 marks)

(c) Look at the results that were obtained from solution **C**.

  (i) Which metal ion is present in the solution? .... (1 mark)

  (ii) Which anion must be present to give fizzing when hydrochloric acid is added to solution **C**? .... (1 mark)

(d) Using the information in the table, give the formula of the chemical present in each of the solutions.

  (i) solution **A** ....

  (ii) solution **B** ....

  (iii) solution **C** .... (3 marks)

■ Exam focus

1 Ammonia is a gas, NH_3, which is manufactured by the Haber process. It has many uses, including the production of nitric acid and the production of many important ammonium salts.

   (a) Which chemicals are the feedstock for the Haber process?

   .... [2]

   (b) Ammonium sulfate is an important fertiliser. To produce it, ammonia is reacted with sulfuric acid.

   (i) Write a balanced chemical equation for the reaction between ammonia and sulfuric acid to produce ammonium sulfate.

   .... [3]

   (ii) What is the maximum mass of ammonium sulfate which could be formed when 49 g of sulfuric acid is completely reacted with ammonia?

   [4]

   (iii) When this experiment was carried out in the laboratory, only 40 g of ammonium sulfate was produced. What was the percentage yield of the experiment?

   [2]

   [Total: 11]

2 Gaseous ammonia is manufactured in large quantities. The process by which it is manufactured was developed by Fritz Haber in 1911 and used industrially in 1913. The production of this important chemical is affected both by the temperature and by the pressure at which the process is run. The equation which represents the synthesis of ammonia is:

$$N_2(g) + 3H_2(g) \rightleftharpoons 2NH_3(g)$$

An iron catalyst is used.

The graph below shows how the percentage yield of ammonia changes with temperature and pressure.

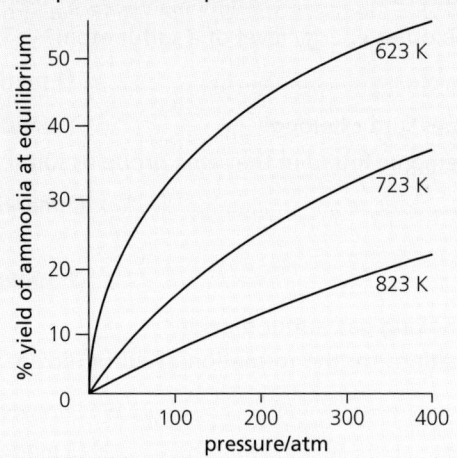

(a) Using the graph, state:
   (i) the effect of increasing the pressure on the yield of ammonia
   .... [2]
   (ii) the effect of decreasing the temperature on the yield of ammonia.
   .... [1]

(b) Explain why the change you have described in part (a) (i) occurs with increasing pressure.
   ....
   .... [3]

(c) Using your answer to part (a) (ii), deduce the sign of the energy change which occurs during the production of ammonia. Explain your answer.
   ....
   .... [3]

(d) The conditions used in industry for the production of ammonia are a pressure of 200 atmospheres and a temperature of 723 K. What is the percentage yield of ammonia under these conditions?
   .... [1]

(e) Why is a temperature lower than 723 K not used?
   ....
   .... [2]

[Total: 12]

16 Sulfur

1. Sulfur has an atomic number of 16 and is represented as:

    $^{32}_{16}S$

    (a) How many electrons are there in a sulfur atom? .... (1 mark)

    (b) How many neutrons are there in a sulfur atom? .... (1 mark)

    (c) How many electrons will there be in the outer energy level of a sulfur atom?

    .... (1 mark)

    (d) To which group of the periodic table does sulfur belong? .... (1 mark)

    (e) Write down the names of two other elements found in the same group as sulfur.

    .... (2 marks)

    (f) Give two large-scale uses for sulfur.

    .... (2 marks)

2. When sulfur is burned in air, it forms the choking gas, sulfur dioxide.

    (a) Write word and balanced chemical equations for the formation of sulfur dioxide.

    ....

    .... (3 marks)

    (b) Complete the bonding diagram for sulfur dioxide shown below. Only the outer energy levels are shown.

    O   S   O

    (4 marks)

    (c) What type of bonding is present in sulfur dioxide?

    .... (1 mark)

3. (a) Rainwater is naturally acidic.

    (i) Explain why this is the case.

    .... (2 marks)

    (ii) What is the expected pH of naturally acidic rainwater?

    .... (1 mark)

    (iii) Another acid is found in rain, which is caused by human activity producing oxides of nitrogen. Give the name and formula of this acid.

    .... (2 marks)

    (b) In many parts of the world, the pH of rainwater has fallen to a lower value.

    (i) What is the pH of acid rain in many parts of the world?

    .... (1 mark)

    (ii) Give two problems associated with acid rain.

    .... (2 marks)

4 The scheme below shows some reactions of dilute sulfuric acid.

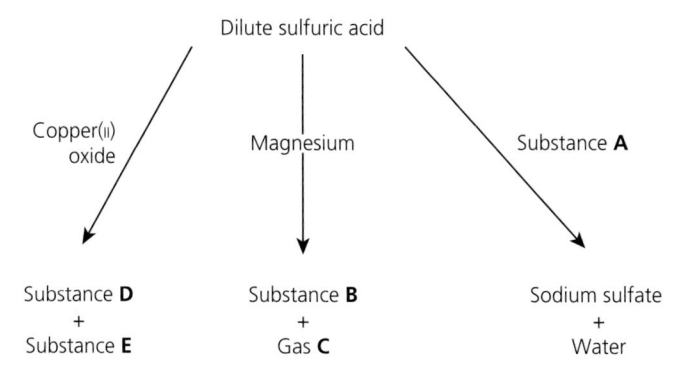

```
                    Dilute sulfuric acid
                  /         |         \
         Copper(II)     Magnesium    Substance A
          oxide
            |              |              |
            ↓              ↓              ↓
        Substance D    Substance B    Sodium sulfate
            +              +              +
        Substance E      Gas C          Water
```

(a) Name and give the formulae of substances **A** to **E**.

A .... (2 marks)

B .... (2 marks)

C .... (2 marks)

D .... (2 marks)

E .... (2 marks)

(b) Write word and balanced chemical equations for the reactions in which substance **A** reacts and substances **B**, **C**, **D** and **E** are formed.

....

....

....

....

....

.... (9 marks)

(c) Describe a chemical test to confirm the identity of gas **C**.

....

.... (2 marks)

5 There are two different sodium salts for sulfuric acid.

   (a) Sodium sulfate is a *normal salt*. What does this term mean?

   ....

   .... (2 marks)

   (b) Describe a chemical test which could be used to show that an unknown substance was a soluble sulfate.

   ....

   .... (3 marks)

   (c) (i) Name and give the formula of a further sodium salt of sulfuric acid, commonly known as an *acid salt*.

   .... (2 marks)

   (ii) What does the term *acid salt* mean?

   ....

   .... (2 marks)

6 Sodium sulfide is a yellow to red colour, and its main use is in the paper industry. It is an ionic solid with the formula Na_2S.

   (a) Draw electronic structures of the ions created when the compound is formed, showing the electrons in the outer energy levels only.

   (4 marks)

   (b) Give three properties which you might expect for this substance, given its bonding.

   ....

   .... (3 marks)

   (c) (i) Would you expect this substance to conduct electricity in the molten state?

   .... (1 mark)

   (ii) Explain your answer.

   .... (2 marks)

7 For each of the following statements, write either 'true' or 'false'.

   (a) Sulfur is a metallic element. .... (1 mark)

   (b) Sulfur reacts with burning magnesium to form magnesium sulfide. .... (1 mark)

   (c) Initially when sulfur dioxide dissolves in rainwater it forms sulfurous acid.

   .... (1 mark)

   (d) Concentrated sulfuric acid cannot remove the water of crystallisation from $CuSO_4.5H_2O$. .... (1 mark)

   (e) In medicine, magnesium sulfate is used as a laxative. .... (1 mark)

   (f) The formation of SO_3 in the Contact process is a reversible reaction.

   .... (1 mark)

8 Draw lines to link each substance on the left with the correct description on the right.

| (a) H$_2$S$_2$O$_7$ |
| (b) CaSO$_4$ |
| (c) SO$_2$ |
| (d) KHSO$_4$ |
| (e) MAZIT metals |
| (f) BaSO$_4$ |
| (g) Concentrated H$_2$SO$_4$ |

A	Formed when testing for a sulfate
B	A powerful dehydrating agent
C	Will react with dilute sulfuric acid
D	A main cause of acid rain
E	Used in making detergents
F	A normal salt of sulfuric acid
G	An acid salt

(7 marks)

Stretch and challenge

9 The real acidity in acid rain is mainly caused by sulfuric acid. The amount of this acid can be determined by carrying out a titration. The results below came from a titration of a sample of acid rain with sodium hydroxide solution. The neutralisation reaction taking place is:

$$H_2SO_4(aq) + 2NaOH(aq) \rightarrow Na_2SO_4(aq) + H_2O(l)$$

25.00 cm³ of acid rain was just neutralised by 15.00 cm³ of a 0.10 mol dm⁻³ sodium hydroxide solution. Calculate:

(a) the concentration of sulfuric acid in the acid rain solution

(3 marks)

(b) the amount of sulfuric acid in 1000 litres of acid rain.

(3 marks)

(c) Acid rain (mainly sulfuric acid) attacks steel structures (mainly iron). Write word and balanced chemical equations for the reaction that takes place.

....

.... (3 marks)

Stretch and challenge

10 Car body parts are made from sheet steel. Before the car body parts are painted, the metal must be free from rust, Fe_2O_3. To ensure that the steel is rust free, the sheets are dipped into sulfuric acid. An unbalanced chemical equation for this process is:

$Fe_2O_3(s) + H_2SO_4(aq) \rightarrow Fe_2(SO_4)_3(aq) + H_2O(l)$

(a) Balance the chemical equation above.

.... (2 marks)

(b) The steel sheets are only left in the acid for a short time. Why are they not left in for longer?

....

.... (3 marks)

(c) Sulfuric acid is used in the manufacture of the fertiliser, $(NH_4)_2SO_4$. What is the name of this substance?

.... (1 mark)

(d) To make the fertiliser in part **(c)**, sulfuric acid has to be neutralised by an alkaline substance. In this case, a possible alkaline substance to use is ammonia solution, NH_4OH.

  (i) Explain what you understand by the term *neutralised* with respect to this reaction.

  ....

  ....

  .... (3 marks)

  (ii) The balanced chemical equation for the reaction between ammonium hydroxide and sulfuric acid is:

  $2NH_4OH(aq) + H_2SO_4(aq) \rightarrow (NH_4)_2SO_4(aq) + 2H_2O(l)$

  Calculate the amount of ammonium sulfate fertiliser produced from 196 tonnes of sulfuric acid. (A_r values: H = 1; C = 12; N = 14; O = 16)

(4 marks)

■ Exam focus

1 When manufacturing sulfuric acid, sulfur dioxide is first made into sulfur trioxide.

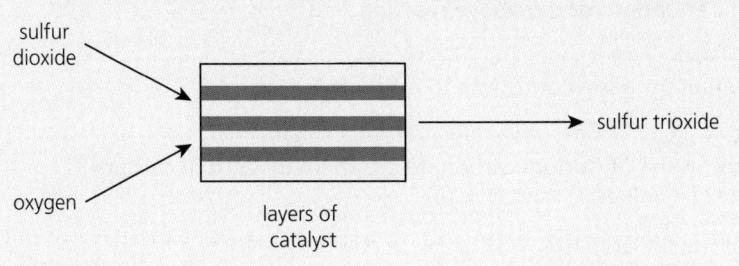

   sulfur dioxide → [layers of catalyst] → sulfur trioxide
   oxygen ↗

   (a) Give two reasons why a catalyst is used in this reaction.

   ....

   .... [3]

   (b) Name and give the formula of the catalyst used in this process.

   .... [2]

   (c) Write word and balanced chemical equations for the making of sulfur trioxide.

   ....

   .... [4]

   (d) The reaction in part (c) goes almost to completion. What does this mean with respect to this reaction?

   ....

   .... [2]

   (e) The sulfur trioxide produced is then dissolved in concentrated sulfuric acid.

   $SO_3(g) + H_2SO_4(l) \rightarrow H_2S_2O_7(l)$

   (i) Give the name of the substance $H_2S_2O_7$.

   .... [1]

   (ii) Why is sulfur trioxide not dissolved directly into water to form concentrated sulfuric acid?

   ....

   ....

   .... [2]

   (f) With the aid of a balanced chemical equation, explain how concentrated sulfuric acid is made from $H_2S_2O_7$.

   ....

   .... [4]

   (g) Give two uses for concentrated sulfuric acid.

   .... [2]

   [Total: 20]

2 It has been found in recent years that the sulfuric acid in acid rain reacts with limestone, which is eaten away by the following process.

$$CaCO_3(s) + H_2SO_4(aq) \rightarrow CaSO_4(s) + H_2O(l) + CO_2(g)$$

(a) Write the ionic equation for the above reaction.

.... [3]

(b) What other pollutant gases contribute to acid rain?

.... [1]

(c) (i) How many moles of calcium carbonate are there in 150 g of calcium carbonate? (A_r values: C = 12; O = 16)

[3]

(ii) Calculate the mass of carbon dioxide formed when 150 g of calcium carbonate reacts with excess sulfuric acid.

[3]

(iii) The amount of sulfuric acid in rainwater has increased over the years. Explain the reasons for this.

....

....

.... [3]

[Total: 13]

Past exam questions

1 All about matter

1 The diagram shows models of various elements.

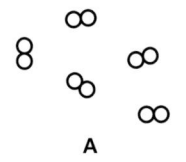

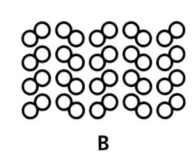

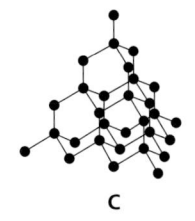

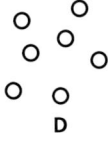

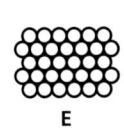

(a) Define the term *element*.

....

.... [1]

(b) Which **one** of the models **A** to **E** represents a solid containing diatomic molecules?

.... [1]

(c) Which **two** of the models **A** to **E** represent gases?

.... and .... [1]

(d) (i) Which **one** of the models **A** to **E** represents diamond?

.... [1]

   (ii) State the name of the element present in diamond.

.... [1]

   (iii) State a use of diamond other than in jewellery.

.... [1]

(e) Structure **E** is a metal. State **three** physical properties which are characteristic of all metals.

....

....

.... [3]

151

(f) Metals are sometimes mixed with other elements in order to change their properties.
  (i) What is the name given to a mixture of metals with other elements?
  .... [1]

  (ii) Match up the metals in the boxes on the left with their uses on the right. The first one has been done for you.

Metal	Use
tin	for making chemical plants
mild steel	for plating tin cans
stainless steel	for car bodies
aluminium	for electrical wiring in houses
copper	for aircraft bodies

  (tin is linked to "for plating tin cans")

  [4]

  [Total: 14]

(Cambridge IGCSE Chemistry 0620, Paper 02 Q 1 June 2006)

2 Elements, compounds and mixtures

2 The following table gives information about six substances.

substance	melting point/°C	boiling point/°C	electrical conductivity as a solid	electrical conductivity as a liquid
A	839	1484	good	good
B	−210	−196	poor	poor
C	776	1497	poor	good
D	−117	78	poor	poor
E	1607	2227	poor	poor
F	−5	102	poor	good

(a) Which substance could have a macromolecular structure similar to that of silicon(IV) oxide?

.... [1]

(b) Which substances are solids at room temperature?

.... [1]

(c) Which substance could be a metal?

.... [1]

(d) Which substance could be aqueous sodium chloride?

.... [1]

(e) Which substance is an ionic compound?

.... [1]

(f) Which substances are liquids at room temperature?

.... [1]

[Total: 6]

(Cambridge IGCSE Chemistry 0620, Paper 32 Q 1 November 2010)

3 Atomic structure and the periodic table

3 The following is a list of the electron distributions of atoms of unknown elements.

element	electron distribution
A	2,5
B	2,8,4
C	2,8,8,2
D	2,8,18,8
E	2,8,18,8,1
F	2,8,18,18,7

(a) Choose an element from the list for each of the following descriptions.

(i) It is a noble gas. ....

(ii) It is a soft metal with a low density. ....

(iii) It can form a covalent compound with element **A**. ....

(iv) It has a giant covalent structure similar to diamond. ....

(v) It can form a negative ion of the type X^{3-}. .... [5]

(b) Elements **C** and **F** can form an ionic compound.

(i) Draw a diagram that shows the formula of this compound, the charges on the ions and the arrangement of the valency electrons around the negative ion.
Use **o** to represent an electron from an atom of **C**.
Use **x** to represent an electron from an atom of **F**.

[3]

(ii) Predict **two** properties of this compound.

....

....

.... [2]

[Total: 10]

(Cambridge IGCSE Chemistry 0620, Paper 31 Q 3 June 2009)

4 Bonding and structure

4 Carbon and silicon are elements in Group IV. Both elements have macromolecular structures.

(a) Diamond and graphite are two forms of the element carbon.
   (i)   Explain why diamond is a very hard substance.

   ....

   ....

   .... [2]

   (ii) Give **one** use for diamond.

   .... [1]

   (iii) Explain why graphite is a soft material.

   ....

   .... [2]

   (iv) Give **one** use of graphite.

   .... [1]

(b) Two of the oxides of these elements are carbon dioxide, CO_2, and silicon(IV) oxide, SiO_2.
   (i)   Draw a diagram showing the arrangement of the valency electrons in one molecule of the covalent compound carbon dioxide.
         Use × to represent an electron from a carbon atom.
         Use ○ to represent an electron from an oxygen atom.

[3]

(ii) A section of the macromolecular structure of silicon(IV) oxide is given below.

Use this diagram to explain why the formula is SiO$_2$ not SiO$_4$.

....

.... [2]

(iii) Predict **two** differences in the physical properties of these two oxides.

....

.... [2]

[Total: 13]

(Cambridge IGCSE Chemistry 0620, Paper 31 Q 5 June 2010)

5 Chemical calculations

5 Quantities of chemicals, expressed in moles, can be used to find the formula of a compound, to establish an equation and to determine reacting masses.

(a) A compound contains 72% magnesium and 28% nitrogen. What is its empirical formula?

....

....

....

.... [2]

(b) A compound contains only aluminium and carbon. 0.03 moles of this compound reacted with excess water to form 0.12 moles of Al(OH)$_3$ and 0.09 moles of CH$_4$. Write a balanced equation for this reaction.

....

....

....

.... [2]

(c) 0.07 moles of silicon reacts with 25 g of bromine.

Si + 2Br$_2$ → SiBr$_4$

(i) Which one is the limiting reagent? Explain your choice.

....

....

....

....

.... [3]

(ii) How many moles of SiBr$_4$ are formed?

.... [1]

[Total: 8]

(Cambridge IGCSE Chemistry 0620, Paper 31 Q 9 June 2009)

6 Electrolysis and its uses

6 Aluminium is extracted by the electrolysis of aluminium oxide.

(a) Hydrated aluminium oxide is heated to produce pure aluminium oxide.

Al$_2$O$_3$.3H$_2$O → Al$_2$O$_3$ + 3H$_2$O
hydrated
aluminium
oxide

What type of reaction is this?
Put a ring around the correct answer.

> **decomposition**   **neutralisation**
> **oxidation**   **reduction**

[1]

(b) Explain why the electrolyte must be molten for electrolysis to occur.

.... [1]

(c) What is the purpose of the cryolite?

.... [1]

(d) Which letter in the diagram, **A**, **B**, **C** or **D**, represents the cathode?

.... [1]

(e) State the name of the products formed at the anode and cathode during this electrolysis.

anode ....

cathode .... [2]

(f) Why do the anodes have to be renewed periodically?

....

.... [2]

(g) Complete the equation for the formation of aluminium from aluminium ions.

Al^{3+} + ... e^- → Al [1]

(h) State one use of aluminium.

.... [1]

[Total: 10]

(Cambridge IGCSE Chemistry 0620, Paper 02 Q 6 November 2009)

7 Acids, bases and salts

7 Oxides are classified as acidic, basic, neutral and amphoteric.

(a) Complete the table.

type of oxide	pH of solution of oxide	example
acidic		
basic		
neutral		

[6]

(b) (i) Explain the term *amphoteric*.

....

.... [1]

(ii) Name two reagents that are needed to show that an oxide is amphoteric.

....

.... [2]

[Total: 9]

(Cambridge IGCSE Chemistry 0620, Paper 31 Q 2 November 2009)

8 Inorganic carbon chemistry

8 Calcium carbonate, $CaCO_3$, is the raw material used in the manufacture of lime, CaO.

  (a) (i) Describe how lime is manufactured from calcium carbonate.

  .... [1]

  (ii) Write a symbol equation for this reaction.

  [1]

  (iii) State one large scale use of lime.

  .... [1]

(b) A student investigated the speed of reaction of calcium carbonate with hydrochloric acid using the apparatus shown below.

  (i) Complete the labelling of the apparatus by filling in the three boxes. [3]

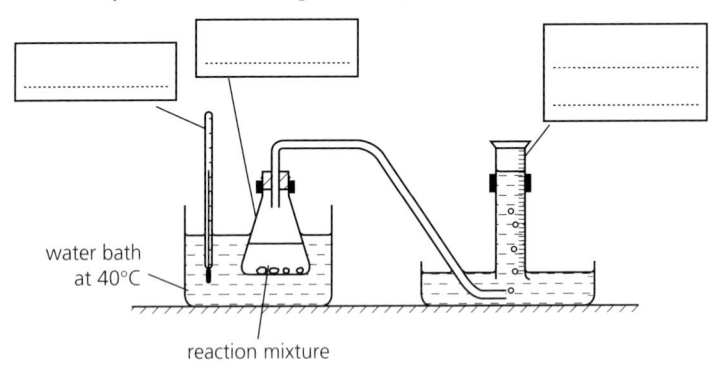

  water bath at 40°C

  reaction mixture

  (ii) The equation for the reaction is

  $$CaCO_3 + 2HCl \rightarrow CaCl_2 + CO_2 + H_2O$$

  Write the word equation for this reaction.

  [2]
  [Total: 8]

  (Cambridge IGCSE Chemistry 0620, Paper 02 Q 3 November 2008)

9 Metal extraction and chemical reactivity

9. Iron is extracted from its ore in a blast furnace.

   (a) State the name of the ore from which iron is extracted.

   .... [1]

   (b) The diagram shows a blast furnace.

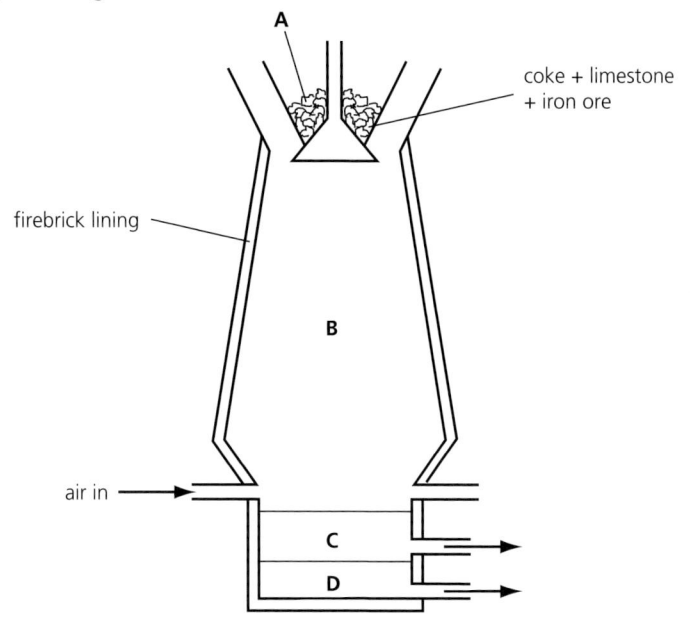

   (i) Which **one** of the raw materials is added to the blast furnace to help remove the impurities from the iron ore?

   .... [1]

   (ii) The impurities are removed as a slag. Which letter on the diagram shows the slag?

   .... [1]

   (c) Carbon monoxide is formed in the blast furnace by reaction of coke with oxygen.

   (i) Complete the equation for this reaction.

   .... C + ... → .... CO   [2]

   (ii) State the adverse affect of carbon monoxide on human health.

   .... [1]

(d) In the hottest regions of the blast furnace the following reaction takes place.

$$Fe_2O_3 + 3C \rightarrow 2Fe + 3CO$$

Which two of these sentences correctly describe this reaction?
Tick **two** boxes.

The iron oxide gets reduced. ☐

The reaction is a thermal decomposition. ☐

The carbon gets oxidised. ☐

The carbon gets reduced. ☐

Carbon neutralises the iron oxide. ☐ [1]

(e) Aluminium cannot be extracted from aluminium oxide in a blast furnace. Explain why aluminium cannot be extracted in this way.

....

.... [2]

(f) (i) State the name of the method used to extract aluminium from its oxide ore.

.... [1]

(ii) State one use of aluminium.

.... [1]

[Total: 11]

(Cambridge IGCSE Chemistry 0620, Paper 02 Q 4 November 2008)

10 Atmosphere and oceans

10 (a) The major gases in unpolluted air are 78% nitrogen and 20% oxygen.
  (i) Name another gaseous element in unpolluted air.

.... [1]

  (ii) Name **two** compounds in unpolluted air.

.... [2]

(b) Two common pollutants in air are carbon monoxide and the oxides of nitrogen.
  (i) Name another pollutant in air.

.... [1]

  (ii) Describe how carbon monoxide is formed.

....

....

.... [2]

(iii) How are the oxides of nitrogen formed?

....

....

.... [2]

(iv) Explain how a catalytic converter reduces the emissions of these two gases.

....

....

.... [2]

[Total: 10]

(Cambridge IGCSE Chemistry 0620, Paper 31 Q 1 November 2009)

11 Rates of reaction

11 Hydrogen peroxide decomposes slowly at room temperature to form water and oxygen.

The reaction is catalysed by manganese(IV) oxide.

$2H_2O_2 \rightarrow 2H_2O + O_2$

A student used the apparatus shown below to study how changing the concentration of hydrogen peroxide affects the speed of this reaction.

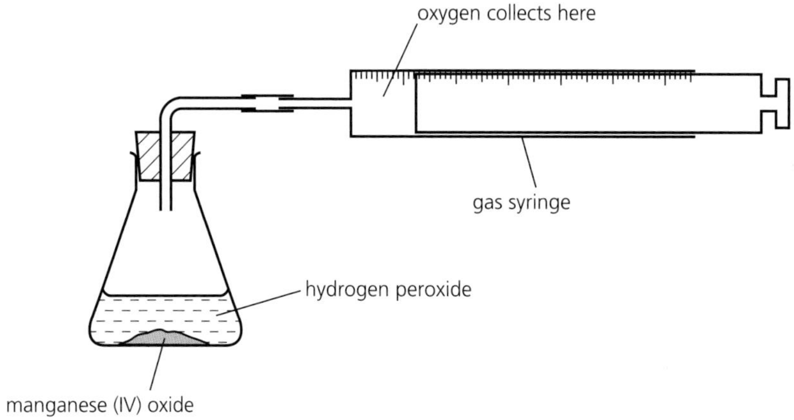

(a) Apart from the volume of hydrogen peroxide, state two things that the student must keep the same in each experiment.

1. ....

2. .... [2]

(b) The student measured the volume of oxygen produced using three different concentrations of hydrogen peroxide.

The results are shown on the graph below.

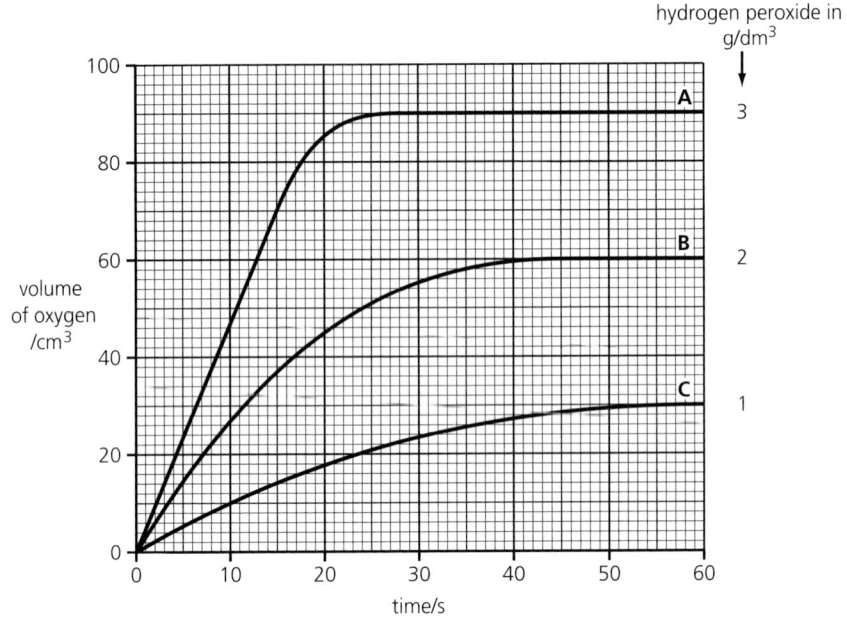

(Graph: volume of oxygen /cm³ vs time/s, showing three curves A (3 g/dm³) levelling at ~90 cm³, B (2 g/dm³) levelling at ~60 cm³, C (1 g/dm³) levelling at ~30 cm³. Concentration of hydrogen peroxide in g/dm³.)

(i) Describe how the speed of the reaction varies with the concentration of hydrogen peroxide.

.... [1]

(ii) Explain why the final volume of oxygen given off is less for graph **B** than for graph **A**.

....

.... [1]

(iii) From the graph, determine

the time taken for the reaction to be completed when 3 g/dm³ hydrogen peroxide (line **A**) was used.

.... [1]

the volume of oxygen produced by 2 g/dm³ hydrogen peroxide (line **B**) in the first 15 seconds.

.... [1]

(c) The student then tested various compounds to see how well they catalysed the reaction. He used the same concentration of hydrogen peroxide in each experiment. The table shows the time taken to produce 20 cm3 of oxygen using each compound as a catalyst.

compound	time taken to produce 20 cm³ of oxygen/s
copper(II) oxide	130
lead(IV) oxide	15
magnesium oxide	did not produce any oxygen
manganese(IV) oxide	18

Put these compounds in order of their effectiveness as catalysts.

worst catalyst ⟶ best catalyst

☐ ☐ ☐ ☐ [1]

[Total: 7]

(Cambridge IGCSE Chemistry 0620, Paper 22 Q 3 November 2011)

12 The petroleum industry

12 Petroleum is a mixture of hydrocarbons which can be separated into fractions such as petrol, paraffin and diesel.

(a) State the name of the process used to separate these fractions.

.... [1]

(b) Name **two** other fractions which are obtained from petroleum.

.... and .... [2]

(c) Give **one** use for the paraffin fraction.

.... [1]

(d) Many of the compounds obtained from petroleum are alkanes. Which **two** of the following structures are alkanes?

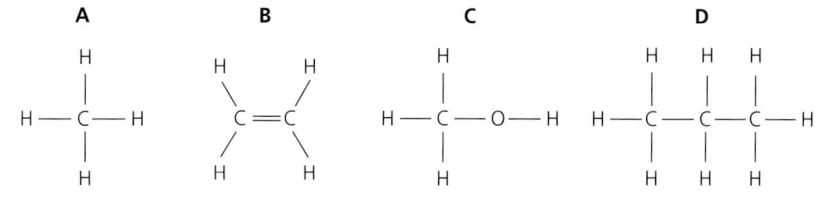

A: CH_4
B: C_2H_4 (C=C with H's)
C: CH_3OH
D: C_3H_8

.... [1]

(e) Use words from the list below to complete the following sentence.

| ethane ethene hydrogen nitrogen |
| oxygen reactive unreactive water |

Alkanes such as .... are generally

.... but they can be burnt in

.... to form carbon dioxide and

.... [4]

(f) Alkanes are saturated hydrocarbons.
What do you understand by the terms

(i) saturated ....

....

(ii) hydrocarbon? ....

.... [2]

[Total: 11]

(Cambridge IGCSE Chemistry 0620, Paper 02 Q 3 June 2009)

13 Energy sources

13 The diagram shows a simple cell.

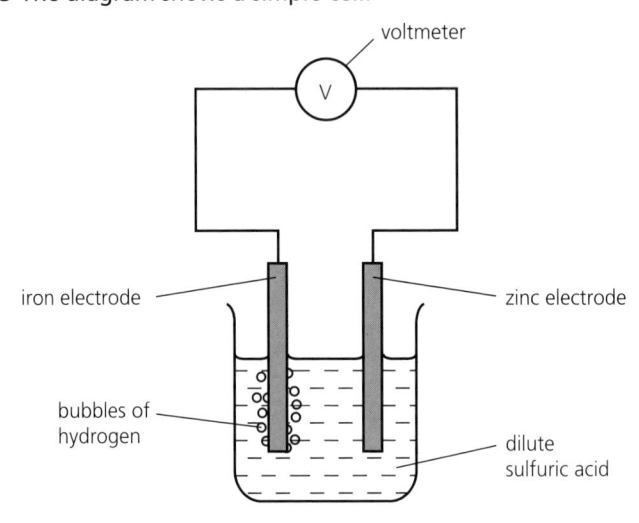

(a) Write an equation for the overall reaction occurring in the cell.

.... [2]

(b) Explain why all cell reactions are exothermic and redox.

....

....

.... [3]

(c) Which electrode, zinc or iron, is the negative electrode? Give a reason for your choice.

....

.... [2]

(d) Suggest **two** ways of increasing the voltage of this cell.

....

.... [2]

[Total: 9]

(Cambridge IGCSE Chemistry 0620, Paper 32 Q 5 November 2011)

14 The (wider) organic manufacturing industry

14 Methanoic acid is the first member of the homologous series of carboxylic acids.

(a) Give **two** general characteristics of a homologous series.

....

....

.... [2]

(b) In some areas when water is boiled, the inside of kettles become coated with a layer of calcium carbonate. This can be removed by adding methanoic acid.
   (i) Complete the equation.
   .... HCOOH + CaCO$_3$ → Ca(HCOO)$_2$ + ... + ... [2]
   (ii) Methanoic acid reacts with most metals above hydrogen in the reactivity series.
   Complete the word equation.

   zinc + methanoic acid → .... + ... [2]
   (iii) Aluminium is also above hydrogen in the reactivity series.
   Why does methanoic acid not react with an aluminium kettle?

   ....

   .... [1]

(c) Give the name, molecular formula and empirical formula of the fourth acid in this series.

name .... [1]

molecular formula .... [1]

empirical formula .... [1]

[Total: 10]

(Cambridge IGCSE Chemistry 0620, Paper 31 Q 8 June 2010)

15 Nitrogen

15 Ammonium sulfate is used in fertilisers.

(a) State the names of the three elements found in most fertilisers.

1. ....

2. ....

3. .... [3]

(b) Suggest why farmers use fertilisers.

....

.... [2]

(c) Ammonium sulfate is a salt which is soluble in water.

(i) What do you understand by the term *soluble*?

.... [1]

(ii) Which of the following methods is used to make this salt in the laboratory?

Tick **one** box.

adding an acid to a metal ☐

adding an acid to a metal oxide ☐

by a precipitation reaction ☐

by the titration of an acid with an alkali ☐ [1]

(d) A mixture of ammonium sulfate and sodium hydroxide was warmed in a test-tube. A gas was given off which turned red litmus paper blue.

State the name of this gas.

.... [1]

(e) Fertilisers containing ammonium salts are often slightly acidic.

(i) State the name of a compound which farmers add to the soil to make it less acidic.

.... [1]

(ii) Explain why it is important for farmers to control the acidity of the soil.

....

.... [2]

(f) The formula of ammonium sulfate is $(NH_4)_2SO_4$.
In this formula state:
(i) the number of different types of atoms present, [1]
(ii) the total number of atoms present. [1]

[Total: 13]

(Cambridge IGCSE Chemistry 0620, Paper 21 Q 5 June 2010)

16 Sulfur

16 (a) Sulfuric acid is made by the Contact process.

$$2SO_2 + O_2 \rightleftharpoons 2SO_3$$

This is carried out in the presence of a catalyst at 450 °C and 2 atmospheres pressure.

(i) How is the sulfur dioxide made?

....

.... [1]

(ii) Give another use of sulfur dioxide.

.... [1]

(iii) Name the catalyst used.

.... [1]

(iv) If the temperature is decreased to 300 °C, the yield of sulfur trioxide increases. Explain why this lower temperature is not used.

....

.... [1]

(v) Sulfur trioxide is dissolved in concentrated sulfuric acid. This is added to water to make more sulfuric acid. Why is sulfur trioxide not added directly to water?

....

.... [1]

(b) Sulfuric acid was first made in the Middle East by heating the mineral, green vitriol, $FeSO_4 \cdot 7H_2O$. The gases formed were cooled.

$$FeSO_4 \cdot 7H_2O(s) \rightarrow FeSO_4(s) + 7H_2O(g)$$
green crystals   yellow powder
$$2FeSO_4(s) \rightarrow Fe_2O_3(s) + SO_2(g) + SO_3(g)$$

On cooling
$$SO_3 + H_2O \rightarrow H_2SO_4 \quad \text{sulfuric acid}$$
$$SO_2 + H_2O \rightarrow H_2SO_3 \quad \text{sulfurous acid}$$

(i) How could you show that the first reaction is reversible?

....

.... [2]

(ii) Sulfurous acid is a reductant. What would you see when acidified potassium manganate(VII) is added to a solution containing this acid?

....

.... [2]

(iii) Suggest an explanation why sulfurous acid in contact with air changes into sulfuric acid.

.... [1]

(c) 9.12 g of anhydrous iron(II) sulfate was heated. Calculate the mass of iron(III) oxide formed and the volume of sulfur trioxide, at r.t.p., formed.

$$2FeSO_4(s) \rightarrow Fe_2O_3(s) + SO_2(g) + SO_3(g)$$

mass of one mole of $FeSO_4$ = 152 g

number of moles of $FeSO_4$ used = ...

number of moles of Fe_2O_3 formed = ...

mass of one mole of Fe_2O_3 = ... g

mass of iron(III) oxide formed = ... g

number of moles of SO_3 formed = ...

volume of sulfur trioxide formed = ... dm³   [6]

[Total: 16]

(Cambridge IGCSE Chemistry 0620, Paper 31 Q 6 November 2009)